Workshop on Peoples Web Meets NLP: Collaboratively Constructed Semantic Resources 2009

(Peoples Web 2009)

Held at ACL-IJCNLP 2009

Singapore
7 August 2009

ISBN: 978-1-61738-455-4

Printed from e-media with permission by:

Curran Associates, Inc.
57 Morehouse Lane
Red Hook, NY 12571

Some format issues inherent in the e-media version may also appear in this print version.

Printed by Curran Associates, Inc. (2010)

Association for Computational Linguistics
209 N. Eighth Street
Stroudsburg, Pennsylvania 18360

Phone: 1-570-476-8006
Fax: 1-570-476-0860

acl@aclweb.org

Additional copies of this publication are available from:

Curran Associates, Inc.
57 Morehouse Lane
Red Hook, NY 12571 USA
Phone: 845-758-0400
Fax: 845-758-2634
Email: curran@proceedings.com
Web: www.proceedings.com

Preface

Welcome to the proceedings of the ACL Workshop "The People's Web Meets NLP: Collaboratively Constructed Semantic Resources". The workshop attracted 21 submissions, of which 9 are included in these proceedings. We are gratified by this level of interest.

This workshop was motivated by the observation that the NLP community is currently considerably influenced by online resources, which are collaboratively constructed by ordinary users on the Web. In many works, such resources have been used as semantic resources overcoming the knowledge acquisition bottleneck and coverage problems pertinent to conventional lexical semantic resources. The resource that has gained the greatest popularity in this respect so far is Wikipedia. However, the scope of the workshop deliberately exceeded Wikipedia. We are happy that the proceedings include papers on resources such as Wiktionary, Mechanical Turk, or creating semantic resources through online games. This encourages us in our belief that collaboratively constructed semantic resources are of growing interest for the natural language processing community.

We should also add that we hoped to bring together researchers from both worlds: those using collaboratively created resources in NLP applications and those using NLP applications for improving the resources or extracting different types of semantic information from them. This is also reflected in the proceedings, although the stronger interest was taken in using semantic resources for NLP applications.

We thank the Volkswagen Foundation and the German Research Foundation for supporting the workshop.

Iryna Gurevych and Torsten Zesch

Organizers:

Iryna Gurevych, Technische Universität Darmstadt
Torsten Zesch, Technische Universität Darmstadt

Program Committee:

Delphine Bernhard, Technische Universität Darmstadt
Paul Buitelaar, DERI, National University of Ireland, Galway
Razvan Bunescu, University of Texas at Austin
Pablo Castells, Universidad Autnonoma de Madrid
Philipp Cimiano, Delft University of Technology
Irene Cramer, Dortmund University of Technology
Andras Csomai, Google Inc.
Ernesto De Luca, University of Magdeburg
Roxana Girju, University of Illinois at Urbana-Champaign
Andreas Hotho, University of Kassel
Graeme Hirst, University of Toronto
Ed Hovy, University of Southern California
Jussi Karlgren, Swedish Institute of Computer Science
Boris Katz, Massachusetts Institute of Technology
Adam Kilgarriff, Brighton, Lexical Computing Ltd, UK
Chin-Yew Lin, Microsoft Research
James Martin, University of Colorado Boulder
Olena Medelyan, University of Waikato
David Milne, University of Waikato
Saif Mohammad, University of Maryland
Dan Moldovan, University of Texas at Dallas
Kotaro Nakayama, University of Tokyo
Ani Nenkova, University of Pennsylvania
Guenter Neumann, DFKI Saarbrücken
Maarten de Rijke, University of Amsterdam
Magnus Sahlgren, Swedish Institute of Computer Science
Manfred Stede, Potsdam University
Benno Stein, Bauhaus University Weimar
Tonio Wandmacher, University of Osnabrück
Rene Witte, Concordia University Montral
Hans-Peter Zorn, European Media Lab, Heidelberg

Invited Speaker:

Rada Mihalcea, University of North Texas

Sponsors:

Volkswagen Foundation as part of the Lichtenberg-Professorship Program under grant No. I/82806 and German Research Foundation (DFG) under grant 798/1-3.

Table of Contents

A Novel Approach to Automatic Gazetteer Generation using Wikipedia
Ziqi Zhang and Jose Iria 1

Named Entity Recognition in Wikipedia
Dominic Balasuriya, Nicky Ringland, Joel Nothman, Tara Murphy and James R. Curran 10

Wiktionary for Natural Language Processing: Methodology and Limitations
Emmanuel Navarro, Franck Sajous, Bruno Gaume, Laurent Prévot, ShuKai Hsieh, Ivy Kuo, Pierre Magistry and Chu-Ren Huang 19

Using the Wiktionary Graph Structure for Synonym Detection
Timothy Weale, Chris Brew and Eric Fosler-Lussier 28

Automatic Content-Based Categorization of Wikipedia Articles
Zeno Gantner and Lars Schmidt-Thieme 32

Evaluating a Statistical CCG Parser on Wikipedia
Matthew Honnibal, Joel Nothman and James R. Curran 38

Construction of Disambiguated Folksonomy Ontologies Using Wikipedia
Noriko Tomuro and Andriy Shepitsen 42

Acquiring High Quality Non-Expert Knowledge from On-Demand Workforce
Donghui Feng, Sveva Besana and Remi Zajac 51

Constructing an Anaphorically Annotated Corpus with Non-Experts: Assessing the Quality of Collaborative Annotations
Jon Chamberlain, Udo Kruschwitz and Massimo Poesio 57

Conference Program

Friday, August 7, 2009

8:45–9:00 Opening Remarks

09:00–09:30 *A Novel Approach to Automatic Gazetteer Generation using Wikipedia*
Ziqi Zhang and Jose Iria

09:30–10:00 *Named Entity Recognition in Wikipedia*
Dominic Balasuriya, Nicky Ringland, Joel Nothman, Tara Murphy and James R. Curran

10:00–10:30 Coffee Break

10:30–11:00 *Wiktionary for Natural Language Processing: Methodology and Limitations*
Emmanuel Navarro, Franck Sajous, Bruno Gaume, Laurent Prévot, ShuKai Hsieh, Ivy Kuo, Pierre Magistry and Chu-Ren Huang

11:00–11:20 *Using the Wiktionary Graph Structure for Synonym Detection*
Timothy Weale, Chris Brew and Eric Fosler-Lussier

11:20–11:40 *Automatic Content-Based Categorization of Wikipedia Articles*
Zeno Gantner and Lars Schmidt-Thieme

11:40–12:00 *Evaluating a Statistical CCG Parser on Wikipedia*
Matthew Honnibal, Joel Nothman and James R. Curran

12:10–13:50 Lunch Break

13:50–14:50 Invited Talk by Rada Mihalcea

15:00–15:30 *Construction of Disambiguated Folksonomy Ontologies Using Wikipedia*
Noriko Tomuro and Andriy Shepitsen

15:30–16:00 Coffee Break

16:00–16:20 *Acquiring High Quality Non-Expert Knowledge from On-Demand Workforce*
Donghui Feng, Sveva Besana and Remi Zajac

Friday, August 7, 2009 (continued)

16:20–16:40 *Constructing an Anaphorically Annotated Corpus with Non-Experts: Assessing the Quality of Collaborative Annotations*
Jon Chamberlain, Udo Kruschwitz and Massimo Poesio

16:40–17:00 Discussion

A Novel Approach to Automatic Gazetteer Generation using Wikipedia

Ziqi Zhang
University of Sheffield, UK
z.zhang@dcs.shef.ac.uk

José Iria
University of Sheffield, UK
j.iria@dcs.shef.ac.uk

Abstract

Gazetteers or entity dictionaries are important knowledge resources for solving a wide range of NLP problems, such as entity extraction. We introduce a novel method to automatically generate gazetteers from seed lists using an external knowledge resource, the Wikipedia. Unlike previous methods, our method exploits the rich content and various structural elements of Wikipedia, and does not rely on language- or domain-specific knowledge. Furthermore, applying the extended gazetteers to an entity extraction task in a scientific domain, we empirically observed a significant improvement in system accuracy when compared with those using seed gazetteers.

1 Introduction

Entity extraction is the task of identifying and classifying atomic text elements into predefined categories such as person names, place names, and organization names. Entity extraction often serves as a fundamental step for complex Natural Language Processing (NLP) applications such as information retrieval, question answering, and machine translation. It has been recognized that in this task, gazetteers, or entity dictionaries, play a crucial role (Roberts et al, 2008). In addition, they serve as important resources for other studies, such as assessing level of ambiguities of a language, and disambiguation (Maynard et al, 2004).

Because building and maintaining high quality gazetteers by hand is very time consuming (Kazama and Torisawa, 2008), many solutions have proposed generating gazetteers automatically from existing resources. In particular, the success that solutions which exploit Wikipedia[1] have been enjoying in many other NLP applications has encouraged a number of research works on automatic gazetteer generation to use Wikipedia, such as works by Toral and Muñoz (2006), and Kazama and Torisawa (2007).

Unfortunately, current systems still present several limitations. First, none have exploited the full content and structure of Wikipedia articles, but instead, only make use of the article's first sentence. However, the full content and structure of Wikipedia carry rich information that has been proven useful in many other NLP problems, such as document classification (Gabrilovich and Markovitch, 2006), entity disambiguation (Bunescu and Paşca, 2006), and semantic relatedness (Strube and Ponzetto, 2006). Second, no other works have evaluated their methods in the context of entity extraction tasks. Evaluating these generated gazetteers in real NLP applications is important, because the quality of these gazetteers has a major impact on the performance of NLP applications that make use of them. Third, the majority of approaches focus on newswire domain and the four classic entity types location (LOC), person (PER), organization (ORG) and miscellaneous (MISC), which have been studied extensively. However, it has been argued that entity extraction is often much harder in scientific domains due to complexity of domain languages, density of information and specificity of classes (Murphy et al, 2006; Byrne, 2007; Nobata et al, 2000).

In this paper we propose a novel approach to automatically generating gazetteers using external knowledge resources. Our method is language- and domain- independent, and scalable. We show that the content and various structural elements of Wikipedia can be successfully exploited to generate high quality gazetteers. To assess gazetteer quality, we evaluate it in the context of entity extraction in the scientific domain of Archaeology, and demonstrate that the generated gazetteers improve the performance of an SVM-based entity tagger across all entity types on an archaeological corpus.

The rest of the paper is structured as follows. In the next section, we review related work. In section 3 we explain our methodology for auto-

[1] http://en.wikipedia.org

Proceedings of the 2009 Workshop on the People's Web Meets NLP, ACL-IJCNLP 2009, pages 1–9,
Suntec, Singapore, 7 August 2009.

matic gazetteer generation. Section 4 introduces the problem domain and describes the experiments conducted. Section 5 presents and discusses the results. Finally we conclude with an outline of future work.

2 Related Work

Currently, existing methods to automatic gazetteer generation can be categorized into two mainstreams; *pattern driven approach* and *knowledge resource approach*.

The *pattern driven approach* uses domain- and language specific patterns to extract candidate entities from unlabeled corpora. The idea is to include features derived from unlabeled data to improve a supervised learning model. For example, Riloff and Jones (1999) introduced a bootstrapping algorithm which starts from seed lists and, iteratively learns and refines domain specific extraction patterns for a semantic category that are then used for building dictionaries from unlabeled data. Talukdar et al (2006), also starting with seed entity lists, apply pattern induction to an unlabeled corpus and then use the induced patterns to extract candidate entities from the corpus to build extended gazetteers. They showed that using the token membership feature with the extended gazetteer improved the performance of a Conditional Random Field (CRF) entity tagger; Kozareva (2006) designed language specific extraction patterns and validation rules to build Spanish location (LOC), person (PER) and organization (ORG) gazetteers from unlabeled data, and used these to improve a supervised entity tagger.

However, the *pattern driven approach* has been criticized for weak domain adaptability and inadequate extensibility due to the specificity of derived patterns. (Toral and Muñoz, 2006; Kazama and Torisawa, 2008). Also, often it is difficult and time-consuming to develop domain- and language-specific patterns.

The *knowledge resource approach*, attempts to solve these problems by relying on the abundant information and domain-independent structures in existing large-scale knowledge resources. Magnini et al (2002) used WordNet as a gazetteer together with rules to extract entities such as LOC, PER and ORG. They used two relations in WordNet; Word_Class, referring to concepts bringing external evidence; and Word_Instance, referring to particular instances of those concepts. Concepts belonging to Word_Class are used to identify trigger words for candidate entities in corpus, while concepts of Word_Instance are used directly as lookup dictionaries. They achieved good results on a newswire corpus. The main limitation of WordNet is lack of domain specific vocabulary, which is critical to domain specific applications (Schütze and Pedersen, 1997). Roberts et al (2008) used terminology extracted from UMLS as gazetteers and tested it in an entity extraction task over a medical corpus. Contrary to WordNet, UMLS is an example of a domain specific knowledge resource, thus its application is also limited.

Recently, the exponential growth in information content in Wikipedia has made this Web resource increasingly popular for solving a wide range of NLP problems and across different domains.

Concerning automatic gazetteer generation, Toral and Muñoz (2006) tried to build gazetteers for LOC, PER, and ORG by extracting all noun phrases from the first sentences of Wikipedia articles. Next they map the noun phrases to WorldNet synsets, and follow the hyperonymy hierarchy until they reach a synset belonging to the entity class of interest. However, they did not evaluate the generated gazetteers in the context of entity extraction. Due to lack of domain specific knowledge in WordNet, their method is limited if applied to domain specific gazetteer generation. In contrast, our method overcomes this limitation since it doesn't rely on any resources other than Wikipedia. Another fundamental difference is that our method exploits more complex structures of Wikipedia.

Kazama and Torisawa (2007) argued that while traditional gazetteers map word sequences to predefined entity categories such as "London → {LOCATION}", a gazetteer is useful as long as it returns consistent labels even if these are not predefined categories. Following this hypothesis, they mapped Wikipedia article titles to their hypernyms by extracting the first noun phrase after *be* in the first sentence of the article, and used these as gazetteers in an entity extraction task. In their experiment, they mapped over 39,000 search candidates to approximately 1,200 hypernyms; and using these hypernyms as category labels in an entity extraction task showed an improvement in system performance. Later, Kazama and Torisawa (2008) did the same in another experiment on a Japanese corpus and achieved consistent results. Although novel, their method in fact bypasses the real problem of generating gazetteers of specific entity types. Our method is essentially different in this aspect. In addition, they only use the first sentence of Wikipedia articles.

3 Automatic Gazetteer Generation – the Methodology

In this section, we describe our methodology for automatic gazetteer generation using the *knowledge resource approach.*

3.1 Wikipedia as the knowledge resource

To demonstrate the validity of our approach, we have selected the English Wikipedia as the external knowledge resource. Wikipedia is a free multilingual and collaborative online encyclopedia that is growing rapidly and offers good quality of information (Giles, 2005). Articles in Wikipedia are identified by unique names, and refer to specific entities. Wikipedia articles have many useful structures for knowledge extraction; for example, articles are inter-connected by hyperlinks carrying relations (Gabrilovich and Markovitch, 2006); articles about similar topics are categorized under the same labels, or grouped in lists; categories are organized as taxonomies, and each category is associated with one or more parent categories (Bunescu and Paşca, 2006). These relations are useful for identifying related articles and thus entities, which is important for automatic gazetteer generation. Compared to other knowledge resources such as WordNet and UMLS, Wikipedia covers significantly larger amounts of information across different domains, therefore, it is more suitable for building domain-specific gazetteers. For example, as of February 2009, there are only 147,287 unique words in WordNet[2], whereas the English Wikipedia is significantly larger with over 2.5 million articles. A study by Holloway (2007) identified that by 2005 there were already 78,977 unique categories divided into 1,069 disconnected category clusters, which can be considered as the same number of different domains.

3.2 The methodology

We propose an automatic gazetteer generation method using Wikipedia article contents, hyperlinks, and category structures, which can generate entity gazetteers of any type. Our method takes input seed entities of any type, and extends them to more complete lists of the same type. It is based on three hypotheses;

1. Wikipedia contains articles about domain specific seed entities.
2. Using articles about the seed entities, we can extract fine-grained *type labels* for them, which can be considered as a list of hypernyms of the seed entities, and predefined entity type hyponyms of the seeds.
3. Following the links on Wikipedia articles, we can reach a large collection of articles that are related to the source articles. If a related article's *type label* (as extracted above) matches any of those extracted for seed entities, we consider it a similar entity of the predefined type.

Naturally, we divide our methods into three steps; firstly we match a seed entity to a Wikipedia article (the matching phase); next we label seed entities using the articles extracted for them and build a pool of fine-grained *type labels* for the seed entities (the labeling phase); finally we extract similar entities by following links in articles of seed entities (the expansion phase). The pseudo-algorithm is illustrated in Figure 1.

3.2.1 Matching seed entities to Wikipedia article

For a given seed entity, we firstly use the exact phrase to retrieve Wikipedia articles. If not found, we use the leftmost longest match, as done by Kazama and Torisawa (2007). In Wikipedia, searches for ambiguous phrases are redirected to a Disambiguation Page, from which users have to manually select a sense. We filter out any matches that are directed to disambiguation pages. This filtering strategy is also applied to step 3 in extracting candidate entities.

3.2.2 Labeling seed entities

After retrieving Wikipedia articles for all seed entities, we extract fine-grained *type labels* from these articles. We identified two types of information from Wikipedia that can extract potentially reliable labels.

---

[2] According to http://wordnet.princeton.edu/man/wnstats.7WN , February 2009

```
Input: seed entities SE of type T
Output: new entities NE of type T
STEP 1 (section 3.2.1)
  1.1. Initialize Set P as articles for SE;
  1.2. For each entity e: SE
  1.3.    Retrieve Wikipedia article p for e;
  1.4.    Add p to P;
STEP 2 (section 3.2.2)
  2.1. Initialize Set L
  2.2. For each p: P
  2.3.    Extract fine grained type labels l;
  2.4.    Add l to L;
STEP 3 (section 3.2.3)
  3.1. Initialize Set HL;
  3.2. For each p: P
  3.3.    Add hyperlinks from p to HL;
  3.4. If necessary, recursively crawl extracted
       hyperlinks and repeat 3.2 and 3.3
  3.5. For each link hl: HL
  3.6.    Extract fine grained type labels l';
  3.7.    If L contains l'
  3.8.       Add title of hl to NE;
  3.9.       Add titles of redirect links of hl to
```

Figure 1. The proposed pseudo-algorithm for gazetteer generation from the content and various structural elements of Wikipedia

As Kazama and Torisawa (2007) observed, in the first sentence of an article, the head noun of the noun phrase just after *be* is most likely the hypernym of the entity of interest, and thus a good category label. There are two pitfalls to this approach. First, the head noun may be too generic to represent a domain-specific label. For example, following their approach the label extracted for the archaeological term "Classical Stage"[3] from the sentence "The Classic Stage is an *archaeological term* describing a particular developmental level." is "term", which is the head noun of "archaeological term". Clearly in such case the phrase is more domain-specific. For this reason we use the exact noun phrase as category label in our work. Second, their method ignores a correlative conjunction which in most cases indicates equivalently useful labels. For example, the two noun phrases in *italic* in the sentence "Sheffield is a *city* and *metropolitan borough* in South Yorkshire, England" are equally useful labels for the article "Sheffield". Therefore, we also extract the noun phrase connected by a correlative conjunction as the label. We apply this method to articles retrieved in 3.2.1. For simplicity, we refer to this approach to labeling seed entities as ***FirstSentenceLabeling***, and the labels created as L_s. Note that our method is essentially different from Kazama and Torisawa as we do not add these extracted nouns to gazetteers; instead, we only use them for guiding the extraction of candidate entities, as described in section 3.2.3.

As mentioned in section 3.1, similar articles in Wikipedia are manually grouped under the same categories by their authors, and categories are further organized as a taxonomy. As a result, we extract category labels of articles as fine-grained *type labels* and consider them to be hypernyms of the entity's article. We refer to this method as ***CategoryLabeling***, and apply it to the seed entities to create a list of category labels, which we denote by L_c.

Three situations arise in which the ***CategoryLabeling*** introduces noisy labels. First, some articles are categorized under a category with the same title as the article itself. For example, the article about "Bronze Age" is categorized under category "Bronze Age". In this case, we explore the next higher level of the category tree, i.e., we extract categories of the category "Bronze Age", including "2nd Millennium", "3rd millennium BC", "Bronze", "Periods and stages in Archaeology", and "Prehistory". Second, some categories are meaningless and for management purposes, such as "Articles to be Merged since 2008", "Wikipedia Templates". For these, we manually create a small list of "stop" categories to be discarded. Third, according to Strube and Ponzetto (2008), the category hierarchy is sometimes noisy. To reduce noisy labels, we only keep labels that are extracted for at least 2 seed entities.

Once a pool of fine-grained *type labels* have been created, in the next step we consider them as fine-grained and immediate hypernyms of the seed entities, and use them as *control vocabulary* to guide the extraction of candidate entities.

3.2.3 Extracting candidate entities

To extract candidate entities, we first identify from Wikipedia the entities that are related to the seed entities. Then we select from them those candidates that share one or more common hypernyms with the seed entities. The intuition is that in the taxonomy, nodes that share common immediate parents are mostly related, and, therefore, good candidates for extended gazetteers.

[3]Any Wikipedia examples for illustration in this paper make use of the English Wikipedia, February 2009, unless otherwise stated.

We extract related entities by following the hyperlinks from the articles retrieved for the seed entities, as by section 3.2.1. This is because in Wikipedia, articles often contain mentions of entities that also have a corresponding article, and these mentions are represented as outgoing hyperlinks. They link the main article of an entity (*source entity*) to other sets of entities (*related entities*). Therefore, by following these links we can reach a large set of related entities to the seed list. To reduce noise, we also filter out links to disambiguation pages as in section 3.2.1. Next, for each candidate in the related set, we use the two labeling approaches introduced in section 3.2.2 to extract its *type labels*. If any of these are included by the *control vocabulary* built with the same labeling approach, we accept them into the extended gazetteers. That is, if the *control vocabulary* is built by ***FirstSentenceLabeling*** we only use ***FirstSentenceLabeling*** to label the candidate. The same applies to ***CategoryLabeling***. One can easily extend this stage by recursively crawling the hyperlinks contained in the retrieved pages. In addition, some Wikipedia articles have one or more redirecting links, which groups several surface forms of a single entity. For example a search for "army base" is redirected to article "military base". These surface forms can be considered as synonyms, and we thus also select them for extend gazetteers.

After applying the above processes to all seed entity articles, we obtain the output extended gazetteers of domain-specific types. To eliminate potentially ambiguous entities, for each extended gazetteer, we exclude entities that are found in domain-independent gazetteers. For example, we use a generic person name gazetteer to exclude ambiguous person names from the extended gazetteers for LOC.

4 Experiments

In this section we describe our experiments. Our goal is to build extended gazetteers using the methods proposed in section 3, and test them in an entity extraction task to improve a baseline system. First we introduce the setting, an entity extraction task in the archaeological domain; next we describe data preparation including training data annotation and gazetteer generation; then, we introduce our baseline; and finally present the results.

4.1 The Problem Domain

The problem of entity extraction has been studied extensively across different domains, particularly in newswire articles (Talukdar et al 2006), bio-medical science (Roberts et al, 2008). In this experiment, we present the problem within the domain of archaeology, which is a discipline that has a long history of active fieldwork and a significant amount of legacy data dating back to the nineteenth century and earlier. Jeffrey et al (2009) reports that despite the existing fast-growing large corpora, little has been done to develop high quality meta-data for efficient access to information in these datasets, which has become a pressing issue in archaeology. To our best knowledge, three works have piloted the research on using information extraction techniques for automatic meta-data generation in this field. Greengrass et al (2008) applied entity and relation extraction to historical court records to extract names, locations and trial names and their relations; Amrani et al (2008) used a series of text-mining technologies to extract archaeological knowledge from specialized texts, one of these tasks concerns entity extraction. Byrne (2007) applied entity and relation extraction to a corpus of archaeology site records. Her work concentrated on nested entity recognition of 11 entity types.

Our work deals with archaeological entity extraction from un-structured legacy data, which mostly consist of full-length archaeological reports varying from 5 to over a hundred pages. According to Jeffrey et al (2009), three types of entities are most useful to an archaeologist;

- Subject (SUB) – topics that reports refer to, such as findings of artifacts and monuments. It is the most ambiguous type because it covers various specialized domains such as warfare, architecture, agriculture, machinery, and education. For example "Roman pottery", "spearhead", and "courtyard".
- Temporal terms (TEM) – archaeological dates of interest, which are written in a number of ways, such as years "1066 - 1211", "circa 800AD"; centuries "C11", "the 1st century"; concepts "Bronze Age", "Medieval"; and acronyms such as "BA" (Bronze Age), "MED" (Medieval).
- Location (LOC) – place names of interest, such as place names and site addresses related to a finding or excavation. In our study, these refer to UK-specific places.

Source	Domain	Tag Density
astro-ph	Astronomy	5.4%
MUC7	Newswire	11.8%
GENIA	Biomedical	33.8%
AHDS-selected	Archaeology	9.2%

Table 1. Comparison of tag density in four test corpora for entity extraction tasks. The "AHDS-selected" corpus used in this work has a tag density comparable to that of MUC7

4.2 Corpus and resources

We developed and tested our system on 30 full length UK archaeological reports archived by the Arts and Humanities Data Service (AHDS)[4]. These articles vary from 5 to 120 pages, with a total of 225,475 words. The corpus is tagged by three archaeologists, and is used for building and testing the entity extraction system. Compared to other test data reported in Murphy et al (2006), our task can be considered hard, due to the heterogeneity of information of the entity types and lower tag density in the corpus (the percentage of words tagged as entities), see Table 1. Also, according to Vlachos (2007), full length articles are harder than abstracts, which are found common in biomedical domain. This corpus is then split into five equal parts for a five-fold cross validation experiment.

For seed gazetteers, we used the MIDAS Period list[5] as the gazetteer for TEM, the Thesaurus of Monuments Types (TMT2008) from English Heritage[6] and the Thesaurus of Archaeology Objects from the STAR project[7] as gazetteers for SUB, and the UK Government list of administrative areas as the gazetteer for LOC. In the following sections, we will refer to these gazetteers as *GAZ_original*.

4.3 Automatic gazetteer generation

We used the seed gazetteers together with the methods presented in section 3 to build new gazetteers for each entity type, and merge them with the seeds as extended gazetteers to be tested in our experiments. Since we introduced two methods for labeling seed entities (section 3.2.2), which are also used separately for selecting extracted candidate entities (section 3.2.3), we design four experiments to test the methods separately as well as in combination; specifically for each entity type, $GAZ\_EXT_{firstsent}$ denotes the extended gazetteer built using ***FirstSentenceLabeling*** for labeling seed entities and selecting candidate entities; $GAZ\_EXT_{category}$ refers to the extended gazetteer built with ***CategoryLabeling***; GAZ_EXT_{union} merges entities in two extended gazetteers into a single gazetteer; while $GAZ\_EXT_{intersect}$ is the intersection of $GAZ\_EXT_{firstsent}$ and $GAZ\_EXT_{category}$ i.e., taking only entities that appear in both. Table 2 lists statistics of the gazetteers and Table 3 displays example type labels extracted by the two methods.

To implement the entity extraction system, we used Runes[8] data representation framework, a collection of information extraction modules from T-rex[9], and the machine learning framework Aleph[10]. The core of the tagger system is a SVM classifier. We used the Java Wikipedia Library[11] (JWPL v0.452b) and the Wikipedia dump of Feb 2007 published with it.

4.4 Feature selection and baseline system

We trained our baseline system by tuning feature sets used and the size of the token window to consider for feature generation; and we select the best performing setting as the baseline. Later we add official gazetteers in section 4.1 and extended gazetteers as in section 4.3 to the baselines and use gazetteer membership as an additional feature to empirically verify the improvement in system accuracy.

The baseline setting thus used a window size of 5 and the following feature set:

- Morphological root of a token
- Exact token string
- Orthographic type (e.g., lowercase, uppercase)
- Token kind (e.g., number, word)

4.5 Result

Table 4 displays the results obtained under each setting, using the standard metrics of *Recall (R)*, *Precision (P)* and *F-measure* (*F1*). The bottom row illustrates **I**nter **A**nnotator **A**greement *(IAA)*

[4] http://ahds.ac.uk/

[5] http://www.midas-heritage.info and http://www.fish-forum.info

[6] http://thesaurus.english-heritage.org.uk

[7] http://hypermedia.research.glam.ac.uk/kos/STAR/

[8] http://runes.sourceforge.net/

[9] http://t-rex.sourceforge.net/

[10] http://aleph-ml.sourceforge.net/

[11] http://www.ukp.tu-darmstadt.de/software/jwpl/

	LOC	SUB	TEM
GAZ_original	11,786 (8,228 found)	5,725 (4,320 found)	61 (43 found)
GAZ_EXT $_{firstsent}$	19,385 (7,599)	11,182 (5,457)	163 (102)
GAZ_EXT $_{category}$	18,861 (7,075)	13,480 (7,745)	305 (245)
GAZ_EXT $_{union}$	23,741 (11,955)	16,697 (10,972)	333 (272)
GAZ_EXT $_{intersect}$	14,022 (2,236)	7,455 (1,730)	133 (72)

Table 2. Number of unique entities in each gazetteer, including official and extended versions. GAZ_EXT includes GAZ_original. For GAZ_original, numbers in brackets are the number of entities found in Wikipedia. For others, they are the number of extracted entities that are new to the corresponding GAZ_original

LOC		SUB		TEM	
FirstSentence-Labeling (597)	*CategoryLabeling* (779)	*FirstSentence-Labeling* (1342)	*CategoryLabeling* (761)	*FirstSentence-Labeling* (11)	*CategoryLabeling* (10)
village, small village, place, town, civil parish	villages in north Yorkshire, north Yorkshire geography stubs, villages in Norfolk, villages in Somerset, English market towns	facility, building, ship, tool, device, establishment	ship types, monument types, gardening, fortification, architecture stubs	period, archaeological period, era, century, millennium	Periods and stages in archaeology, Bronze age, middle ages, historical eras, centuries

Table 3. Top 5 most frequently extracted (counted by number of seed entities sharing that label) fine-grained *type labels* for each entity type. Numbers in brackets are the number of unique labels extracted

	LOC			SUB			TEM		
	P	R	F1	P	R	F1	P	R	F1
Baseline (B)	*69.4*	*67.4*	*68.4*	*69.6*	*62.3*	*65.7*	*82.3*	*81.4*	*81.8*
B+ GAZ_original	*69.0*	*72.1*	*70.5*	*69.7*	*65.4*	*67.5*	*82.3*	*82.7*	*82.5*
B+ GAZ_EXT $_{firstsent}$	**69.9**	**76.7**	**73.1**	**70.0**	**68.3**	**69.1**	**82.6**	**84.6**	**83.6**
B+ EXT $_{category}$	**69.1**	**75.1**	**72.0**	68.8	**67.0**	**67.9**	82.0	**83.7**	**82.8**
B+ EXT $_{union}$	68.9	**75.0**	**71.8**	**69.8**	**66.5**	**68.1**	**82.4**	**83.4**	**82.9**
B+ EXT $_{intersect}$	69.3	**76.2**	**72.6**	**69.7**	**67.6**	**68.6**	**82.6**	**84.3**	**83.4**
IAA	-	-	75.3	-	-	63.6	-	-	79.9

Table 4. Experimental results showing accuracy of systems in the entity extraction task for each type of entities, varying the feature set used. Baseline performances are marked in *italic*. Better performances than baselines achieved by our systems are highlighted in *bold*.

between the annotators on a shared sample corpus of the same kind as that for building the system, calculated using the metric by Hripcsak and Rothschild (2005). The metric is equivalent to scoring one annotator against the other using the *F1* metric, and in practice system performance can be slightly higher than *IAA* (Roberts et al, 2008). The *IAA* figures for all types of entities are low, indicating that the entity extraction task for the archaeological domain is difficult, which is consistent with Byrne (2007)'s finding.

5 Discussion

As shown in Table 2, our methods have generated domain specific gazetteers that almost doubled the original seed gazetteers in every occasion, even for the smallest seed gazetteer of TEM. This proves our hypotheses formulated in section 3.1, that by utilizing the hyperonymy relation and exploring information in an external resource, one can extend a gazetteer by entities of similar types without utilizing language- and domain-specific knowledge. Also by taking the intersection of entities generated by the two labeling methods (bottom row of table 2), we see that the overlap is relatively small (from 30%-40% of the list generated by either method), indicating that the extended gazetteers produced by the two methods are quite different, and may be used to complement each other. Combining figures in Table 3, we see that both methods extract fine-grained type-labels that on average extract 4 - 14 candidate entities.

The quality of the gazetteers can be checked using the figures in Table 4. First, all extended gazetteers improved over the baselines for the three entity types, with the highest increase in *F1* of 4.7%, 3.4% and 1.8% for LOC, SUB, and

TEM respectively. In addition, they all outperform the original gazetteers, indicating that the quality of extended gazetteers is good for the entity extraction task.

By comparing the effects of each extended gazetteer, we notice that using the gazetteers built with type-labels extracted from the first sentence of Wikipedia article always outperforms using those built via the Wikipedia categories, indicating that the first method (***FirstSentenceLabeling***) results in better quality gazetteers. This is due to two reasons. First, the category tree in Wikipedia is not a strict taxonomy, and does not always contain *is-a* relationships (Strube and Ponzetto, 2006). Although we have eliminated categories that are extracted for only one seed entity, the results indicate the extended gazetteers are still noisier than those built by ***FirstSentenceLabeling***. To illustrate, the articles for SUB seed entities "quiver" and "arrowhead" are both categorized under "Archery", which permits noisy candidates such as "Bowhunting", "Camel archer" and "archer". Applying a stricter filtering threshold may resolve this problem. Second, compared to Wikipedia categories, the labels extracted from the first sentences are sometimes very fine-grained and restrictive. For example, the labels extracted for "Buckinghamshire" from the first sentence are "ceremonial Home County" and "Non-metropolitan County", both of which are UK-specific LOC concepts. These rather restrictive labels help control the gazetteer expansion within the domain of interest. The better performance with ***FirstSentenceLabeling*** indicates that such restrictions have played a positive role in reducing noise in the labels generated, and then improving the quality of candidate entities.

We also tested effects of combining the two approaches, and noticed that taking the intersection of gazetteers generated by the two approaches outperform the union, but figures are still lower than the single best method. This is understandable because by permitting members of noisier gazetteers the system performance degrades.

6 Conclusion

We have presented a novel language- and domain- independent approach for automatically generating domain-specific gazetteers for entity recognition tasks using Wikipedia. Unlike previous approaches, our approach makes use of richer content and structural elements of Wikipedia. By applying this approach to a corpus of the Archaeology domain, we empirically observed a significant improvement in system accuracy when compared with the baseline systems, and the baselines plus original gazetteers.

The extensibility and domain adaptability of our methods still need further investigation. In particular, our methods can be extended to introduce several statistical filtering thresholds to control the label generation and candidate entity extraction in an attempt to reduce noise; also the effect of recursively crawling Wikipedia articles in the candidate extraction stage is worth studying. Additionally, it would be interesting to study other structures of Wikipedia, such as list structures and info boxes, in gazetteer generation. In future we will investigate into these possibilities, and also test our approach in different domains.

Acknowledgement

This work is funded by the Archaeotools[12] project that is carried out by Archaeology Data Service, University of York, UK and the Organisation, Information and Knowledge Group (OAK) of University of Sheffield, UK.

References

Ahmed Amrani, Vichken Abajian, Yves Kodratoff, and Oriane Matte-Tailliez. 2008. A Chain of Text-mining to Extract Information in Archaeology. In *Proceedings of Information and Communication Technologies: From Theory to Applications, ICT-TA 2008*, 1-5.

Razva Bunescu and Marius Paşca. Using Encyclopedic Knowledge for Named Entity Disambiguation. In *Proceedings of EACL2006*

Kate Byrne. Nested Named Entity Recognition in Historical Archive Text. In *Proceedings of International Conference on Semantic Computing*, 2007.

Evgeniy Gabrilovich and Shaul Markovitch. Overcoming the Brittleness Bottleneck using Wikipedia: Enhancing Text Categorization with Encyclopedic Knowledge. In *Proceedings of the Twenty-First National Conference on Artificial Intelligence*, 1301-1306, Boston, 2006.

Jim Giles. Internet Encyclopedias Go Head to Head. In *Nature 438*. 2005. 900-901.

Mark Greengras, Sam Chapman, Jamie McLaughlin, Ravish Bhagdev and Fabio Ciravegna. Finding Needles in Haystacks: Data-mining in Distributed Historical Datasets. In *The Virtual Representation of the Past*. London, Ashgate. 2008

[12] http://ads.ahds.ac.uk/project/archaeotools/

George Hripcsak and Adam S. Rothschild. Agreement, the F-measure and Reliability in Information Retrieval: In *Journal of the American Medical Informatics Association*, 296-298. 2005

Todd Holloway, Miran Bozicevic and Katy Börner. Analyzing and Visualizing the Semantic Coverage of Wikipedia and its Authors. In *Complexity, Volumn 12, issue 3*, 30-40. 2007

Stuart Jeffrey, Julian Richards, Fabio Ciravegna, Stewart Waller, Sam Chapman and Ziqi Zhang. 2009. The Archaeotools project: Faceted Classification and Natural Language Processing in an Archaeological Context. To appear in *special Theme Issues of the Philosophical Transactions of the Royal Society A,"Crossing Boundaries: Computational Science, E-Science and Global E-Infrastructures"*.

Jun'ichi Kazama and Kentaro Torisawa. 2008. Inducing Gazetteers for Named Entity Recognition by Large-scale Clustering of Dependency Relations. In *Proceedings of ACL-2008: HLT*, 407-415.

Jun'ichi Kazama and Kentaro Torisawa. Exploting Wikipedia as External Knowledge for Named Entity Recognition. In *Proceedings of EMNLP-2007 and Computational Natural Language Learning 2007*. 698-707.

Zornista Kozareva. 2006. Bootstrapping Named Entity Recognition with Automatically Generated Gazetteer Lists. *In EACL-2006-SRW*.

Bernardo Magnini, Matto Negri, Roberto Prevete and Hristo Tanev. AWordNet-Based Approach to Named Entity Recognition. In *Proceedings of COLING-2002 on SEMANET: building and using semantic networks*. 1-7

Diana Maynard, Kalina Bontcheva and Hamish Cunningham. Automatic Language-Independent Induction of Gazetteer Lists. In *Proceedings of LREC2004*.

Tara Murphy, Tara Mcintosh and James R Curran. Named Entity Recognition for Astronomy Literature. In *Proceedings of the Australasian Language Technology Workshop*, 2006.

Chikashi Nobata, Nigel Collier and Jun'ichi Tsujii. Comparison between Tagged Corpora for the Named Entity Task. In Proceedings of the Workshop on Comparing Corpora at ACL2000.

Ellen Riloff and Rosie Jones. 1999. Learning Dictionaries for Information Extraction by Multi-level Bootstrapping. In *Proceedings of the Sixteenth National Conference on Artificial Intelligence*, 474-479.

Angus Roberts, Robert Gaizauskas, Mark Hepple and Yikun Guo. Combining Terminology Resources and Statistical Methods for Entity Recognition: an Evaluation. In *Proceedings of LREC2008*.

Hinrich Schütze and Jan O. Pedersen. A cooccurrence-based thesaurus and two applications to Information Retrieval. In *Information Processing and Management: an International Journal, 1997*. 33(3): 307-318

Michael Strube and Simone Paolo Ponzetto. WikiRelate! Computing Semantic Relatedness Using Wikipedia. In *Proceedings of the 21st National Conference on Artificial Intelligence*, 2006. 1419 - 1424

Partha Pratim Talukdar, Thorsten Brants, Mark Liberman and Fernando Pereira. 2006. A Context Pattern Induction Method for Named Entity Extraction. In *Proceedings of CoNLL-2006,* 141-148.

Antonio Toral and Rafael Muñoz. 2006. A Proposal to Automatically Build and Maintain Gazetteers for Named Entity Recognition by using Wikipedia. In *Proceedings of Workshop on New Text, 11th Conference of the European Chapter of the Association for Computational Linguistics 2006*.

Andreas Vlachos. Evaluating and Combining Biomedical Named Entity Recognition Systems. In *Workshop: Biological translational and clinical language processing*. 2007

Named Entity Recognition in Wikipedia

Dominic Balasuriya Nicky Ringland Joel Nothman Tara Murphy James R. Curran
School of Information Technologies
University of Sydney
NSW 2006, Australia
{dbal7610,nicky,joel,tm,james}@it.usyd.edu.au

Abstract

Named entity recognition (NER) is used in many domains beyond the newswire text that comprises current gold-standard corpora. Recent work has used Wikipedia's link structure to automatically generate near gold-standard annotations. Until now, these resources have only been evaluated on newswire corpora or themselves.

We present the first NER evaluation on a Wikipedia gold standard (WG) corpus. Our analysis of cross-corpus performance on WG shows that Wikipedia text may be a harder NER domain than newswire. We find that an automatic annotation of Wikipedia has high agreement with WG and, when used as training data, outperforms newswire models by up to 7.7%.

1 Introduction

Named Entity Recognition (NER) is the task of identifying and classifying people, organisations and other named entities (NE) within text. NER is central to many NLP systems, especially information extraction and question answering.

Machine learning approaches now dominate NER, learning patterns associated with individual entity classes from annotated training data. This training data, including English newswire from the MUC-6, MUC-7 (Chinchor, 1998), and CoNLL-03 (Tjong Kim Sang and De Meulder, 2003) competitive evaluation tasks, and the BBN Pronoun Coreference and Entity Type Corpus (Weischedel and Brunstein, 2005), is critical to the success of these approaches.

This data dependence has impeded the adaptation or *porting* of existing NER systems to new domains, such as scientific or biomedical text, e.g. Nobata et al. (2000). Similar domain sensitivity is exhibited by most tasks across NLP, e.g. parsing (Gildea, 2001), and the adaptation penalty is still apparent even when the same set of named entity classes is used in text from similar domains (Ciaramita and Altun, 2005).

Wikipedia is an important corpus for information extraction, e.g. Bunescu and Paşca (2006) and Wu et al. (2008) because of its size, currency, rich semi-structured content, and its closer resemblance to web text than newswire. Recently, Wikipedia's markup has been exploited to automatically derive NE annotated text for training statistical models (Richman and Schone, 2008; Mika et al., 2008; Nothman et al., 2008).

However, without a gold standard, existing evaluations of these models were forced to compare against mismatched newswire corpora or the noisy Wikipedia-derived annotations themselves. Further, it was not possible to directly ascertain the accuracy of these automatic extraction methods.

We have manually annotated 39,007 tokens of Wikipedia with coarse-grained named entity tags (WG). We present the first evaluation of Wikipedia-trained models on Wikipedia: the C&C NER tagger (Curran and Clark, 2003b) trained on (a) automatically annotated Wikipedia text (WP2) extracted by Nothman et al. (2009); and (b) traditional newswire NER corpora (MUC, CoNLL and BBN). The WP2 model, though trained on noisy annotations, outperforms newswire models on WG by 7.7%. However, every model, including WP2, performs far worse on WG than on the newswire.

We examined the quality of WG, and found that our annotation strategy produced a high-quality, consistent corpus. Our analysis suggests that it is the form and distribution of NEs in Wikipedia that make it a difficult target domain.

Finally, we compared WG with the annotations extracted by Nothman et al. (2009), and found agreement comparable to our inter-annotator agreement, demonstrating that NE corpora can be derived very accurately from Wikipedia.

Proceedings of the 2009 Workshop on the People's Web Meets NLP, ACL-IJCNLP 2009, pages 10–18,
Suntec, Singapore, 7 August 2009.

2 Background

Traditional evaluations of NER have considered the performance of a tagger on test data from the same source as its training data. Although the majority of annotated corpora available consist of newswire text, recent practical applications cover a far wider range of genres, including Wikipedia, blogs, RSS feeds, and other data sources. Ciaramita and Altun (2005) showed that even when moving a short distance, e.g. annotating WSJ text with the same scheme as CoNLL's Reuters, the performance was 26% worse than on the original text.

Similar differences are reported by Nothman et al. (2009) who compared MUC, CoNLL and BBN annotations reduced to a common tag-set. They found poor cross-corpus performance to be due to tokenisation and annotation scheme mismatch, missing frequent lexical items, and naming conventions. They then compared automatically-annotated Wikipedia text as training data and found it also differs in otherwise inconsequential ways from the newswire corpora, in particular lacking abbreviations necessary to tag news text.

2.1 Automatic Wikipedia annotation

Wikipedia, a collaboratively-written online encyclopedia, is readily exploited in NLP, because it is large, semi-structured and multilingual. Its articles often correspond to NEs, so it has been used for NE recognition (Kazama and Torisawa, 2007) and disambiguation (Bunescu and Paşca, 2006; Cucerzan, 2007). Wikipedia links often span NEs, which may be exploited to automatically create annotated NER training data by determining the entity class of the linked article and then labelling the link text with it.

Richman and Schone (2008) use article classification knowledge from English Wikipedia to produce NE-annotated corpora in other languages (evaluated against NE gold standards for French, Spanish, and Ukrainian). Mika et al. (2008) explored the use of tags from a CoNLL-trained tagger to seed the labelling of entities and evaluate the performance of a Wikipedia-trained model by hand.

We make use of an approach described by Nothman et al. (2009) which is engineered to perform well on BBN data with a reduced tag-set (LOC, MISC, ORG, PER). They derive an annotated corpus with the following steps:

1. Classify Wikipedia articles into entity classes
2. Split the articles into tokenised sentences
3. Label expanded links according to target NEs
4. Select sentences for inclusion in a corpus

To prepare the text, they use `mwlib` (PediaPress, 2007) to parse Wikipedia's native markup retaining only paragraph text with links, apply Punkt (Kiss and Strunk, 2006) estimated on Wikipedia text to perform sentence boundary detection, and tokenise the resulting text using regular expressions.

Nothman et al. (2009) infer additional NEs not provided by existing links, and apply rules to adjust link boundaries and classifications to closer match BBN annotations.

2.2 NER evaluation

Meaningful automatic evaluation of NER is difficult and a number of metrics have been proposed (Nadeau and Sekine, 2007). Ambiguity leads to entities correctly delimited but misclassified, or boundaries mismatched despite correct classification.

Although the MUC-7 evaluation (Chinchor, 1998) defined a metric which was less sensitive to often-meaningless boundary errors, we consider only exact entity matches as correct, following the standard CoNLL evaluation (Tjong Kim Sang, 2002). We report precision, recall and F-score for each entity type.

3 Creating the Wikipedia gold standard

We created a corpus by manually annotating the text of 149 articles from the May 22, 2008 dump of English Wikipedia. The articles were selected at random from all articles describing named entities, with a roughly equal proportion of article topics from each of the four CoNLL-03 classes (LOC, MISC, ORG, PER). We adopted Nothman et al.'s (2008) preprocessing described above to produce tokenised sentences for annotation.

Only body text was extracted from the chosen articles for inclusion in the corpus. Four articles were found not to have any usable text, consisting solely of tables, lists, templates and section headings, which we remove. Their exclusion leaves a corpus of 145 articles.

3.1 Annotation

Annotation was initially carried out using a fine-grained tag-set which was expanded by the an-

[COMPANY Aero Gare] was a kitplane manufacturer founded by [PERSON Gary LeGare] in [CITY Mojave] , [STATE California] to marketed the [PLANE Sea Hawker] amphibious aircraft .

(a) Fine-grained annotation

[ORG Aero Gare] was a kitplane manufacturer founded by [PER Gary LeGare] in [LOC Mojave] , [LOC California] to marketed the [MISC Sea Hawker] amphibious aircraft .

(b) Coarse-grained annotation

Figure 1: An example of coarse and fine-grained annotation of Wikipedia text.

notators as annotation progressed, and eventually contained 96 tags.

We created a mapping from these fine-grained tags to the four coarse-grained tags used in the CoNLL-03 data: PER, LOC, MISC and ORG. This enables evaluation with existing NER models. We believe this two-phase approach allowed annotators to defer difficult mapping decisions, (e.g. should an airport be classified as a LOC, ORG, or MISC?) which can then be made after discussion. The mapping could also be modified to suit a particular evaluation task.

Figure 1 shows an example of the use of fine and coarse-grained tags to annotate a sentence. Tags such as PERSON correspond directly to coarse-grained tags, while most map to a more general tag, such as STATE and CITY mapping to LOC. PLANE is an example of a fine-grained tag that cannot be mapped to LOC, ORG, or PER. These tags may be mapped to MISC; some are not considered entities under the CoNLL scheme and are left unlabelled in the coarse-grained annotation.

Three independent annotators were involved in the annotation process. Annotator 1 annotated all 145 articles using the fine-grained tags. Annotators 2 and 3 then re-annotated 19 of these articles (316 sentences or 8030 tokens), amounting to 21% of the corpus. Annotator 2 used the fine-grained tags described above, while Annotator 3 used the four coarse-grained CoNLL tags. To measure variation, all three annotations of this common portion were mapped down to the CoNLL tag-set and inter-annotator agreement was calculated.

We found that 202 tokens were disagreed upon by at least one annotator (2.5% of all tokens annotated), and these discrepancies were then discussed by the three annotators. The inter-annotator agreement will be analysed in more detail in Section 5.

Sentences containing grammatical and typographical errors were not corrected, so that the corpus would be as close as possible to the source text. Web text often contains errors, such as to

Train	Test	P	R	F
WP2	WG	66.5	67.4	66.9
BBN	WG	59.2	59.1	59.2
CoNLL	WG	54.3	57.2	55.7
WP2 *	WG *	75.1	67.7	71.2
BBN *	WG *	57.2	64.1	60.4
CoNLL *	WG *	53.1	62.7	57.5
MUC *	WG *	52.3	57.2	54.6
WP2	BBN	73.4	74.6	74.0
WP2	CoNLL	73.6	64.9	69.0
WP2 *	MUC *	86.2	68.9	76.6
BBN	BBN	85.7	87.3	86.5
CoNLL	CoNLL	85.3	86.5	85.9
MUC	MUC	81.0	83.6	82.3

Table 2: Tagger performance on various corpora. Asterisks indicate that MISC tags are ignored.

marketed the Sea Hawker from the example in Figure 1, so any NER system must deal with these errors. Sentences with poor tokenisation or sentence boundary detection were identified and corrected manually, since these errors are introduced by our processing and annotation, and do not exist in the source text.

The final corpus was created by correcting annotation mistakes, with annotators 2 and 3 each correcting 50% of the corpus. The fine-grained tags were mapped to the four CoNLL tags before the final corrections were made. The final WG corpus consists of the body text of 145 Wikipedia articles tagged with the four CoNLL-03 tags.

4 NER on the Wikipedia gold-standard

Nothman et al. (2009) have previously shown that that an NER system trained on automatically annotated Wikipedia corpora performs reasonably well on non-Wikipedia text. Having created our WG corpus of gold-standard annotations, we are able to evaluate the performance of these models on Wikipedia text.

We compare the C&C NE maximum-entropy tagger (Curran and Clark, 2003b) trained on gold-standard newswire corpora (MUC-7, BBN and CoNLL-03) with the same tagger trained on automatically annotated Wikipedia text, WP2. WG is

	WG	WP2	BBN		CoNLL-03		MUC-7	
	Test	Train	Train	Test	Train	Test	Train	Test
Tokens	39 007	3 500 032	901 849	129 654	203 621	46 435	83 601	60 436
Sentences	1 696	146 543	37 843	5 462	14 987	3 453	3 485	2 419
Articles	145	—	1 775	238	946	231	102	99
NEs	3 558	288 545	49 999	7 307	23 498	5 648	4 315	3 540

Table 1: Corpus sizes.

too small to train a reasonable NER model on gold-standard Wikipedia annotations. Part-of-speech tags are added to all corpora using the C&C POS tagger (Curran and Clark, 2003a) before training and testing. [1] We evaluate each model on traditional newswire evaluation corpora as well as WG. Table 1 gives the size of each corpus.

The results are shown in Table 2. The WP2 tagger performed substantially better on WG than taggers trained on newswire text, with a 7–11% increase in F-score compared to BBN and CoNLL-03, and a 16% increase compared to MUC-7, when miscellaneous NEs in the corpus are not considered in the evaluation. The Wikipedia trained model thus outperforms newswire models on our new WG corpus even though the training annotations were automatically extracted.

The WP2 tagger performed worse on WG than on gold-standard news corpora (BBN and CoNLL), with a 2–7% reduction in F-score. Further, the performance of WP2 on WG is 11–20% F-score lower than same-source evaluation results, e.g. BBN on BBN, CoNLL on CoNLL. Therefore, despite WP2 showing an advantage in tagging WG due to their common source domain, we find that WG's annotations are harder to predict than the newswire test data commonly used for evaluation.

One possible explanation is that our WG corpus has been inconsistently annotated. When NEs of miscellaneous type are not considered in the evaluation (asterisks in Table 2), the performance of all taggers on WG improves, with WP2 demonstrating a 4% increase. This result suggests another partial explanation: that MISC NEs in Wikipedia are more difficult to annotate correctly, due to their poor definition and broad coverage. A third explanation is that the automatic conversion process proposed by Nothman et al. (2008) produces much lower quality training data than manual annotation. We explore these three possibilities below.

[1] Both taggers are available from http://svn.ask.it.usyd.edu.au/trac/candc.

	Token	Exact	NE only
A1 and A2	0.95	0.99	0.88
A1 and A3	0.91	0.95	0.81
A2 and A3	0.91	0.96	0.79
Fleiss' Kappa	0.92	0.97	0.83

Table 3: Initial human inter-annotator agreement.

5 Quality of the Wikipedia gold standard

The low performance observed on WG may be due to the poor quality of its annotation. We ensure that this is not the case by measuring inter-annotator agreement. The WG annotation process produced three independent annotations of a subset of WG. These annotations were compared using Cohen's κ (Fleiss and Cohen, 1973) between pairs of annotators, and Fleiss' κ (Fleiss, 1971), which generalises Cohen's κ to more than two concurrent annotations.

Table 3 shows the three types of κ values calculated. *Token* is calculated on a per token basis, comparing the agreement of annotators on each token in the corpus; *NE only*, is calculated on the agreement between entities alone, excluding agreement in cases where all annotators agreed that a token was not a NE; *Exact* refers to the agreement between annotators where all annotators have agreed on the boundaries of a NE, but disagree on the type of NE.

Annotator 1 originally annotated the entire corpus, and Annotators 2 and 3 then corrected exactly half of the corpus each after a discussion between the three annotators to resolve ambiguities. Landis and Koch (1977) determine that a κ value greater than 0.81 indicates almost perfect agreement. By this standard, our three annotators were in strong agreement prior to discussion, with our Fleiss' κ values all greater than 0.81. Inconsistencies in the corpus due to annotation mistakes by Annotator 1 were corrected by Annotators 2 and 3.

Inter-annotator agreement for cases where the annotators agreed on NE boundaries was higher than agreement on each token, which suggests that many discrepancies resulted from NE bound-

	LOC	MISC	ORG	PER	$H(C)$: With O	Without O	Total NEs	% NE tokens
WG	28.5	20.0	25.2	26.3	0.98	2.0	3 558	17.1
BBN	22.4	9.8	46.4	21.3	0.61	1.7	49 999	9.6
MUC	33.3	—	40.7	26.1	0.52	1.5	4 315	8.1
CoNLL	30.4	14.6	26.9	28.1	0.98	1.9	23 498	17.1

Table 4: NE class distribution, tag entropy and NE density statistics for gold-standard corpora and WG.

ary ambiguities, or disagreement as to whether a phrase constituted a NE at all. Higher inter-annotator agreement between Annotators 1 and 2 leads us to believe that the two-phase annotation strategy, where an initially fine-grained tag-set is reduced, results in more consistent annotation.

Our analysis demonstrates that WG is annotated in a consistent and accurate manner and the small number of errors cannot alone explain the reduced performance figures.

6 Comparing gold-standard corpora

6.1 NE class distribution

Table 4 compares the distribution of different classes of NEs across different corpora on the four CoNLL categories. WG has a higher proportion of PER and MISC NEs and a lower proportion of ORG NEs than the BBN corpus. This is also found in the MUC corpus, although comparisons to MUC are affected by its lack of a MISC category. The CoNLL-03 corpus is most similar to WG in terms of the distribution of the NE classes, although CoNLL-03 has a smaller proportion of MISC NEs than WG. An analysis of the lengths of NEs in CoNLL shows, however, that they are very different to those in WG (see Table 8), perhaps explaining the difference in performance observed.

Tag entropy $H(C)$ was calculated for each corpus with respect to the 5 possible classes (4 NE classes, and the O tag, indicating non-entities). $H(C)$ is a measure of the amount of information required to represent the classification of each token in the corpus. Two calculations are made, including and excluding the frequent O tag. Our results (Table 4) suggest that WG's tags are least predictable, with a tag entropy of 2.0 bits (without the O class) compared to 1.7 and 1.9 bits for BBN and CoNLL respectively.

6.2 Fine-grained class distribution

While the CoNLL-03 and MUC evaluation corpora are marked up with only very coarse tags, the BBN corpus uses 29 coarse tags, many with specific subtypes, including NEs, descriptors of NEs and non-NEs, intended as answer types for question answering (Brunstein, 2002). Non-NE types include MONEY and TIME, which are also tagged in the MUC corpus, and others such as ANIMAL. When evaluating the performance of the taggers, each of BBN's 150 fine-grained tags was mapped to one of four coarse-grained classes or none, using a mapping described in Nothman (2008).

Mapped BBN tag	WG	BBN
PERSON	25.9	19.3
ORGANIZATION:OTHER	**13.0**	2.8
ORGANIZATION:CORPORATION	9.2	**43.1**
GPE:CITY	8.0	6.7
WORK_OF_ART:SONG	**4.7**	0.1
NORP	4.3	3.1
WORK_OF_ART:OTHER	**4.1**	1.3
GPE:COUNTRY	3.5	5.1
ORGANIZATION:EDUCATIONAL	**3.0**	0.9
GPE:STATE_PROVINCE	2.8	2.8
ORGANIZATION:POLITICAL	**2.6**	0.6
EVENT:OTHER	**2.5**	0.4
ORGANIZATION:GOVERNMENT	2.0	**7.5**
WORK_OF_ART:BOOK	**1.6**	0.4
EVENT:WAR	**1.6**	0.1
FAC:OTHER	**1.4**	0.2
LOCATION:REGION	1.3	0.8
FAC:ATTRACTION	**1.2**	0.0

Table 5: Distribution of some fine-grained tags

However, since the WG corpus was initially annotated using 96 distinct classes, we map these tags to the corresponding fine-grained BBN NE classes. In some cases, the tags map exactly (e.g. COUNTRY mapped to LOCATION:COUNTRY); in other cases, classes have to be merged or not mapped at all, where the BBN and WG annotations differ in granularity. Where possible, we map to fine-grained BBN categories.

We create mappings to a total of 36 BBN entity types, and apply them across the WG corpus. Table 5 shows the distribution of the most common tags, calculated as a percentage of all counts of the 36 selected tags across each corpus. Tags for which there is at least a two-fold difference in proportion between BBN and WG are marked in bold.

The comparison is dominated by the presence of a disproportionate number of ORG:CORPORATIONS in the BBN corpus com-

	1	2	3	4	5	6	7+	# NEs
WG	53.0	77.0	88.9	94.8	96.6	98.2	100	712
BBN (train)	75.0	91.0	95.4	97.2	98.2	98.7	100	4913
CoNLL (train)	75.0	93.8	98.1	99.5	99.9	99.9	100	3437

Table 6: Comparing MISC NE lengths (cumulative).

Feature group	WG	BBN	CoNLL
Current token	0.88	0.89	0.93
Current POS	0.43	0.57	0.48
Current word-type	0.42	0.49	0.48
Previous token	0.46	0.43	0.47
Previous POS	0.12	0.19	0.14
Previous word-type	0.07	0.14	0.12

Table 7: Feature-tag gain ratios.

	1	2	3	4	5	6	7+
WG	49.9	81.7	93.1	97.4	98.6	99.4	100
BBN (train)	57.4	83.3	92.9	97.4	99.1	99.6	100
CoNLL (train)	63.1	94.5	98.4	99.4	99.8	99.9	100
MUC (train)	62.0	89.1	96.1	99.1	99.7	99.8	100

Table 8: Comparing all NE lengths (cumulative).

pared to WG. It also mentions many more governmental organisations. Prominent cases of tags found in higher proportions in WG are works of art, organisations of type OTHER (e.g. bands, sports teams, clubs), events and attractions.

This comparison demonstrates that there are observable differences in NE types between the news and Wikipedia domains. These differences are reflected in the distribution of both coarse and fine-grained types of NEs. The more complex entity distribution in Wikipedia is a likely cause for reduced NER performance on WG.

6.3 Feature-tag gain

Nobata et al. (2000) use *gain ratio* as an information-theoretic measure of corpus difficulty:

$$GR(C;F) = \frac{I(C;F)}{H(C)}$$

where $I(C;F) = H(C) - H(C|F)$ is the information gain of the NE tag distribution (C) with respect to a feature set F.

This gain ratio normalises the information gain over the tag entropy, which Nobata et al. (2000) suggest allows us to compare gain ratios between corpora. It also makes the impact of including the 'O' tag negligible for our calculations.

We apply this approach to measure the relative difficulty of tagging NEs in the WG corpus. Table 7 shows that WG tags seem generally harder to predict than those in newswire, on the basis of words, POS tags or orthographic word-types (like those used in the Curran and Clark (2003b) tagger as proposed by Collins (2002)).

In particular, POS tags are less indicative than in BBN and CoNLL, suggesting a wider variety of grammatical functions in NE names in Wikipedia – this might be expected with more band names, and song and movie titles. Alternatively, it may be an indication that the POS tagging is less reliable on Wikipedia using newswire-trained models.

The previous word's orthographic form also provides less information, which may relate to titles like Mr. and Mrs., strong indicators of PER entities, which are frequent in BBN and to a lesser extent CoNLL, but are almost absent in Wikipedia.

6.4 Lengths of named entities

The number of tokens in NEs is substantially different between WG and other gold-standard corpora. When compared with WG, other gold-standard corpora have a larger proportion of single-word NEs (between 7 and 13% more), as shown in Table 8. The distribution of NE lengths in BBN is most similar to WG, but it still differs significantly in the proportion of single-word NEs.

Additionally, WG has a larger number of long multi-word NEs than the other gold-standard corpora. Longer entities are more difficult to classify, since boundary resolution is more error prone and they typically contain lowercase words with a wider range of syntactic roles. This adds to the difficulty of correctly identifying NEs in WG.

The difference in entity lengths is most pronounced MISC NEs (Table 6), with Wikipedia having a substantially smaller number of single-word MISC NEs. The presence of a large number of long miscellaneous NEs, including song, film and book titles, and other works of art are a feature that characterises the nature of Wikipedia text in contrast to newswire text. Typically, longer MISC NEs in newswire text are laws and NORPs, which also appear in Wikipedia text.

	1	2	3	4	5	6	7+	# NEs
WG	49.2	82.9	94.2	98.0	99.2	99.8	100	2 846
BBN (train)	55.4	82.4	92.6	97.4	99.2	99.7	100	45 086
CoNLL (train)	61.1	94.7	98.4	99.4	99.8	99.9	100	20 061
MUC (train)	62.0	89.1	96.1	99.1	99.7	99.8	100	4 315

Table 9: Comparing non-MISC NE lengths (cumulative).

	# Sents	# with NEs	# NEs
WG	1 696	1 341	3 558
WG WP2-style	571	298	569
WG WP4-style	698	425	831

Table 10: Size of WG and auto-annotated subsets.

TRAIN	TEST	P	R	F
WP2	WG manual	66.5	67.4	66.9
WP2	WG WP2-style	76.0	72.9	74.4
WP2	WG WP4-style	75.5	71.4	73.4
WP2	WP2 ten folds	—	—	83.6
WP2 *	WG manual *	75.1	67.7	71.2
WP2 *	WG WP2-style *	81.5	74.4	77.8
WP2 *	WG WP4-style *	81.9	74.6	78.1
WP2 *	WP2 ten folds *	—	—	86.1

Table 11: NER performance of the WP2-trained model on auto-annotated subsets of WG.

	κ	NE κ	P	R	F
WP2-style	0.94	0.84	89.0	89.0	89.0
WP4-style	0.93	0.83	86.8	87.6	87.2

Table 12: Comparing WP2-style WG and WP4-style WG on WG. The automatically annotated data was treated as predicted annotations on WG.

7 Evaluation of automatic annotation

We compared the gold-standard annotations in our WG corpus to those sentences that were automatically annotated by Nothman et al. (2009). Their automatic annotation process does not retain all Wikipedia sentences. Rather, it selects sentences where, on the basis of capitalisation heuristics, it seems all named entities in the sentence have been tagged by the automatic process. We adopt this confidence criterion to produce automatically-annotated subsets of the WG corpus.

Two variants of their automatic annotation procedure were used: WP2 uses a few rules to infer tags for non-linked NEs in Wikipedia; WP4 has looser criteria for inferring additional links, and its over-generation typically reduced its performance as training data (Nothman et al., 2009).

A large proportion of sentences in our WG corpus cannot be automatically tagged with confidence. Sentence selection leaves 571 sentences (33.7%) after the WP2 process and 698 (41.2%) after the WP4 process (see Table 10). The use of the more permissive WP4 process may lead to the labelling of more NEs, but many may be spurious.

We use three approaches to compare automatic and manual annotations of WG text: (a) treat each corpus as test data and evaluate NER performance on each; (b) treat WP2 and WP4-style subsets as NER predictions on the WG corpus to calculate an F-score; and (c) treat the automatic annotations like human annotators and calculate κ values.

We first evaluate the WP2 model on each corpus and find that performance is higher on automatically-annotated subsets of WG (Table 11). This is unsurprising given the common automatic annotation process and the effects of the selection criterion. However, Nothman (2008) provides an F-score for the WP2 model when evaluated on 10 folds of automatically-annotated (WP2-style) test data. This F-score is 8–10% higher than WP2's performance on the WP2-style subset of WG, suggesting that WG's text is somewhat more difficult to annotate than typical portions of WP2-style text.

We compare the annotations of WG text more directly by treating the automatic annotations as if they are the output from a tagger run on the 698 and 571 sentences that were confidently chosen. A reasonable agreement between the gold standard and automatic annotation is observed (Table 12), with F-scores of 87.2% and 89.0% achieved by WP2 and WP4.

Table 12 also shows inter-annotator agreement calculated between the automatically annotated subsets and the gold-standard annotations in WG, using Cohen's κ in the same way as for human annotators. The agreement was very high: equal or better than the agreement between human annotators prior to discussion and correction.

8 Conclusion

We have presented the first evaluation of named entity recognition (NER) on a gold-standard evaluation of Wikipedia, a resource of increasing importance in Computational Linguistics. We annotated a corpus of Wikipedia articles (WG) with gold-standard NE tags. Using this new resource as test data we have evaluated models trained on three gold-standard newswire corpora for NER, and compared them to a model trained on Wikipedia-derived NER annotations (Nothman et al., 2009). We found that this WP2 model outperformed models trained on MUC, CoNLL, and BBN data by more than 7.7% F-score.

However, we found that all four models performed significantly worse on the WG corpus than they did on news text, suggesting that Wikipedia as a textual domain is more difficult for NER. We initially suspected that annotation quality was responsible, but found that we had very high inter-annotator agreement even before further discussion and correction of the corpus. This also validates our approach of creating many fine-grained categories and then reducing them down to the four CoNLL types.

To further examine the difficulty of tagging WG, we compared the distribution of fine-grained entity types in WG and BBN, finding a more even distribution over a larger range of types in WG. We found that the standard NER features such as current and previous POS tags and words had lower predictive power on WG. We also compared the distribution of NEs lengths and showed that WG entities are longer on average (for instance song and book titles). This all suggests that Wikipedia is genuinely more difficult to automatically annotate with named entities than newswire.

Finally, we compared the common sentences between Nothman et al.'s (2009) automatic NE annotation of Wikipedia and WG, directly measuring the quality of automatically deriving NE annotations from Wikipedia.

We found that WP2 agreed with our final WG corpus to a high degree, demonstrating that Wikipedia is a viable source of automatically annotated NE annotated data, reducing our dependence on expensive manual annotation for training NER systems.

Acknowledgements

We would like to thank the anonymous reviewers for their helpful feedback. This work was supported by the Australian Research Council under Discovery Project DP0665973. Dominic Balasuriya was supported by a University of Sydney Outstanding Achievement Scholarship. Nicky Ringland was supported by a Capital Markets CRC High Achievers Scholarship. Joel Nothman was supported by a Capital Markets CRC PhD Scholarship and a University of Sydney Vice-Chancellor's Research Scholarship.

References

Ada Brunstein. 2002. Annotation guidelines for answer types. LDC2005T33, Linguistic Data Consortium, Philadelphia.

Razvan Bunescu and Marius Paşca. 2006. Using encyclopedic knowledge for named entity disambiguation. In *Proceedings of the 11th Conference of the European Chapter of the Association for Computational Linguistics*, pages 9–16.

Nancy Chinchor. 1998. Overview of MUC-7. In *Proceedings of the 7th Message Understanding Conference.*

Massimiliano Ciaramita and Yasemin Altun. 2005. Named-entity recognition in novel domains with external lexical knowledge. In *Proceedings of the NIPS Workshop on Advances in Structured Learning for Text and Speech Processing.*

Michael Collins. 2002. Ranking algorithms for named-entity extraction: boosting and the voted perceptron. In *Proceedings of the 40th Annual Meeting of the Association for Computational Linguistics*, pages 489–496.

Silviu Cucerzan. 2007. Large-scale named entity disambiguation based on Wikipedia data. In *Proceedings of the 2007 Joint Conference on Empirical Methods in Natural Language Processing and Computational Natural Language Learning*, pages 708–716.

James R. Curran and Stephen Clark. 2003a. Investigating GIS and smoothing for maximum entropy taggers. In *Proceedings of the 10th Conference of the European Chapter of the Association for Computational Linguistics*, pages 91–98, Budapest, Hungary, 12–17 April.

James R. Curran and Stephen Clark. 2003b. Language independent NER using a maximum entropy tagger. In *Proceedings of the 7th Conference on Natural Language Learning*, pages 164–167.

Joseph L. Fleiss and Jacob Cohen. 1973. The equivalence of weighted kappa and the intraclass correlation coefficient as measures of reliability. *Educational and Psychological Measurement*, 33(3):613.

Joseph L. Fleiss. 1971. Measuring nominal scale agreement among many raters. *Psychological Bulletin*, 76(5):378–382.

Daniel Gildea. 2001. Corpus variation and parser performance. In *2001 Conference on Empirical Methods in Natural Language Processing (EMNLP)*, Pittsburgh, PA.

Jun'ichi Kazama and Kentaro Torisawa. 2007. Exploiting Wikipedia as external knowledge for named entity recognition. In *Proceedings of the 2007 Joint Conference on Empirical Methods in Natural Language Processing and Computational Natural Language Learning*, pages 698–707.

Tibor Kiss and Jan Strunk. 2006. Unsupervised multilingual sentence boundary detection. *Computational Linguistics*, 32(4):485–525.

J. Richard Landis and Gary G. Koch. 1977. The measurement of observer agreement for categorical data. *Biometrics*, 33:159–174.

Peter Mika, Massimiliano Ciaramita, Hugo Zaragoza, and Jordi Atserias. 2008. Learning to tag and tagging to learn: A case study on wikipedia. *IEEE Intelligent Systems*, 23(5, Sep./Oct.):26–33.

David Nadeau and Satoshi Sekine. 2007. A survey of named entity recognition and classification. *Lingvisticae Investigationes*, 30:3–26.

Chikashi Nobata, Nigel Collier, and Jun'ichi Tsuji. 2000. Comparison between tagged corpora for the named entity task. In *Proceedings of the Workshop on Comparing Corpora*, pages 20–27.

Joel Nothman, James R Curran, and Tara Murphy. 2008. Transforming Wikipedia into named entity training data. In *Proceedings of the Australasian Language Technology Association Workshop 2008*, pages 124–132, Hobart, Australia, December.

Joel Nothman, Tara Murphy, and James R. Curran. 2009. Analysing Wikipedia and gold-standard corpora for NER training. In *Proceedings of the 12th Conference of the European Chapter of the ACL (EACL 2009)*, pages 612–620, Athens, Greece, March.

Joel Nothman. 2008. *Learning Named Entity Recognition from Wikipedia*. Honours Thesis. School of IT, University of Sydney.

PediaPress. 2007. `mwlib` MediaWiki parsing library. `http://code.pediapress.com`.

Alexander E. Richman and Patrick Schone. 2008. Mining wiki resources for multilingual named entity recognition. In *Proceedings of the 46th Annual Meeting of the Association for Computational Linguistics: Human Language Technologies*, pages 1–9, Columbus, Ohio.

Erik F. Tjong Kim Sang and Fien De Meulder. 2003. Introduction to the CoNLL-2003 shared task: Language-independent named entity recognition. In *Proceedings of the 7th Conference on Natural Language Learning*, pages 142–147, Edmonton, Canada.

Erik F. Tjong Kim Sang. 2002. Introduction to the CoNLL-2002 shared task: Language-independent named entity recognition. In *Proceedings of the 6th Conference on Natural Language Learning*, pages 1–4, Taipei, Taiwan.

Ralph Weischedel and Ada Brunstein. 2005. *BBN Pronoun Coreference and Entity Type Corpus*. LDC2005T33, Linguistic Data Consortium, Philadelphia.

Fei Wu, Raphael Hoffmann, and Daniel S. Weld. 2008. Information extraction from Wikipedia: Moving down the long tail. In *Proceedings of the 14th International Conference on Knowledge Discovery & Data Mining*, Las Vegas, USA, August.

Wiktionary and NLP: Improving synonymy networks

Emmanuel Navarro
IRIT, CNRS &
Université de Toulouse
navarro@irit.fr

Franck Sajous
CLLE-ERSS, CNRS &
Université de Toulouse
sajous@univ-tlse2.fr

Bruno Gaume
CLLE-ERSS & IRIT, CNRS &
Université de Toulouse
gaume@univ-tlse2.fr

Laurent Prévot
LPL, CNRS &
Université de Provence
laurent.prevot@lpl-aix.fr

Hsieh ShuKai
English Department
NTNU, Taiwan
shukai@gmail.com

Kuo Tzu-Yi
Graduate Institute of Linguistics
NTU, Taiwan
tzuyikuo@ntu.edu.tw

Pierre Magistry
TIGP, CLCLP, Academia Sinica,
GIL, NTU, Taiwan
pmagistry@gmail.com

Huang Chu-Ren
Dept. of Chinese and Bilingual Studies
Hong Kong Poly U. , Hong Kong.
churenhuang@gmail.com

Abstract

Wiktionary, a satellite of the Wikipedia initiative, can be seen as a potential resource for Natural Language Processing. It requires however to be processed before being used efficiently as an NLP resource. After describing the relevant aspects of Wiktionary for our purposes, we focus on its structural properties. Then, we describe how we extracted synonymy networks from this resource. We provide an in-depth study of these synonymy networks and compare them to those extracted from traditional resources. Finally, we describe two methods for semi-automatically improving this network by adding missing relations: (i) using a kind of semantic proximity measure; (ii) using translation relations of Wiktionary itself.

Note: The experiments of this paper are based on Wiktionary's dumps downloaded in year 2008. Differences may be observed with the current versions available online.

1 Introduction

Reliable and comprehensive lexical resources constitute a crucial prerequisite for various NLP tasks. However their building cost keeps them rare. In this context, the success of the Princeton WordNet (PWN) (Fellbaum, 1998) can be explained by the quality of the resource but also by the lack of serious competitors. Widening this observation to more languages only makes this observation more acute. In spite of various initiatives, costs make resource development extremely slow or/and result in non freely accessible resources. Collaborative resources might bring an attractive solution to this difficult situation. Among them Wiktionary seems to be the perfect resource for building computational mono-lingual and multi-lingual lexica. This paper focuses therefore on Wiktionary, how to improve it, and on its exploitation for creating resources.

In next section, we present some relevant information about Wiktionary. Section 3 presents the lexical graphs we are using and the way we build them. Then we pay some attention to evaluation (§4) before exploring some tracks of improvement suggested by Wiktionary structure itself.

2 Wiktionary

As previously said, NLP suffers from a lack of lexical resources, be it due to the low-quality or non-existence of such resources, or to copyrights-related problems. As an example, we consider French language resources. Jacquin et al. (2002) highlighted the limitations and inconsistencies from the French EuroWordnet. Later, Sagot and Fišer (2008) explained how they needed to recourse to PWN, BalkaNet (Tufis, 2000) and other resources (notably Wikipedia) to build WOLF, a free French WordNet that is promising but still a very preliminary resource. Some languages are straight-off purely under-resourced.

The *Web as Corpus* initiative arose (Kilgarriff and Grefenstette, 2003) as an attempt to design tools and methodologies to use the web for *overcoming data sparseness* (Keller and Lapata, 2002). Nevertheless, this initiative raised non-trivial technical problems described in Baroni et al. (2008). Moreover, the web is not structured enough to easily and massively extract semantic relations.

In this context, Wiktionary could appear to be a paradisiac playground for creating various lexi-

Proceedings of the 2009 Workshop on the People's Web Meets NLP, ACL-IJCNLP 2009, pages 19–27,
Suntec, Singapore, 7 August 2009.

cal resources. We describe below the Wiktionary resource and we explain the restrictions and problems we are facing when trying to exploit it. This description may complete few earlier ones, for example Zesch et al. (2008a).

2.1 Collaborative editing

Wiktionary, the lexical companion to Wikipedia, is *a collaborative project to produce a free-content multilingual dictionary.*[1] As the other Wikipedia's satellite projects, the resource is not experts-led, rather filled by any kind of users. The might-be inaccuracy of the resulting resource has lengthily been discussed and we will not debate it: see Giles (2005) and Britannica (2006) for an illustration of the controversy. Nevertheless, we think that Wiktionary should be less subject (so far) than Wikipedia to voluntary misleading content (be it for ideological, commercial reasons, or alike).

2.2 Articles content

As one may expect, a Wiktionary article[2] may (not systematically) give information on a word's part of speech, etymology, definitions, examples, pronunciation, translations, synonyms/antonyms, hypernyms/hyponyms, etc.

2.2.1 Multilingual aspects

Wiktionary's multilingual organisation may be surprising and not always meet one's expectations or intuitions. Wiktionaries exist in 172 languages, but we can read on the English language main page, *"1,248,097 entries with English definitions from over 295 languages"*. Indeed, a given wiktionary describes the words in its own language but also foreign words. For example, the English article *moral* includes the word in English (adjective and noun) and Spanish (adjective and noun) but not in French. Another example, *boucher*, which does not exist in English, is an article of the English wiktionary, dedicated to the French noun *(a butcher)* and French verb *(to cork up)*.

A given wiktionary's *'in other languages'* left menu's links, point to articles in other wiktionaries describing the word in the current language. For example, the *Français* link in the *dictionary* article of the English wiktionary points to an article in the French one, describing the English word *dictionary*.

[1] `http://en.wiktionary.org/`

[2] What *article* refers to is more fuzzy than classical *entry* or *acceptance* means.

2.2.2 Layouts

In the following paragraph, we outline wiktionary's general structure. We only consider words in the wiktionary's own language.

An entry consists of a graphical form and a corresponding article that is divided into the following, possibly embedded, sections:

• **etymology** sections separate homonyms when relevant;

• among an etymology section, different **parts of speech** may occur;

• **definitions** and **examples** belong to a part of speech section and may be subdivided into **subsenses**;

• **translations**, **synonyms/antonyms** and **hypernyms/hyponyms** are linked to a given part of speech, with or without subsenses distinctions.

In figure 1 is depicted an article's layout example.

Figure 1: Layout of *boot* article (shortened)

About subsenses, they are identified with an index when first introduced but they may appear as a plain text semantic feature (without index) when used in relations (translations, synonyms, etc.). It is therefore impossible to associate the relations arguments to subsenses. Secondly, subsense index appears only in the current word (the source of the relation) and not in the target word's article it is linked to (see *orange* French N. and Adj., Jan. 10, 2008[3]).

A more serious issue appears when relations are shared by several parts of speech sections. In Ital-

[3] `http://fr.wiktionary.org/w/index.php?title=orange&oldid=2981313`

ian, both synonyms and translations parts are common to all words categories (see for example *cardinale* N. and Adj., Apr. 26, 2009[4]).

2.3 Technical issues

As Wikipedia and the other Wikimedia Foundation's projects, the Wiktionary's content management system relies on the MediaWiki software and on the wikitext. As stated in Wikipedia's MetaWiki article, *"no formal syntax has been defined"* for the MediaWiki and consequently it is not possible to write a 100% reliable parser.

Unlike Wikipedia, no HTML dump is available and one has to parse the Wikicode. Wikicode is difficult to handle since wiki templates require handwritten rules that need to be regularly updated. Another difficulty is the language-specific encoding of the information. Just to mention one, the target language of a translation link is identified by a 2 or 3 letters ISO-639 code for most languages. However in the Polish wiktionary the complete name of the language name (*angielski*, *francuski*, ...) is used.

2.4 Parsing and modeling

The (non-exhaustive) aforementioned list of difficulties (see §2.2.2 and §2.3) leads to the following consequences:

• Writing a parser for a given wiktionary is possible only after an in-depth observation of its source. Even an intensive work will not prevent all errors as long as (i) no syntax-checking is made when editing an article and (ii) flexibility with the "tacitly agreed" layout conventions is preserved. Better, *flexibility* is presented as a characteristic of the framework:

> *"[...] it is not a set of rigid rules. You may experiment with deviations, but other editors may find those deviations unacceptable, and revert those changes. They have just as much right to do that as you have to make them.*[5]"

Moreover, a parser has to be updated every new dump, as templates, layout conventions (and so on) may change.

• Writing parsers for different languages is not a simple adjustment, rather a complete overhaul.

• When extracting a network of semantic relations from a given wiktionary, some choices are more driven by the wiktionary inner format than scientific modelling choices. An illustration follows in §3.2. When merging information extracted from several languages, the homogenisation of the data structure often leads to the choice of the poorest one, resulting in a loss of information.

2.5 The bigger the better?

Taking advantage of colleagues mastering various languages, we studied the wiktionary of the following languages: French, English, German, Polish and Mandarin Chinese. A first remark concerns the size of the resource. The official number of declared articles in a given wiktionary includes a great number of meta-articles which are not word entries As of April 2009, the French wiktionary reaches the first rank[6], before the English one. This can be explained by the automated import of public-domain dictionaries articles (*Littré 1863* and *Dictionnaire de l'Académie Française 1932-1935*). Table 1 shows the ratio between the total number of articles and the "relevant" ones (numbers based on year 2008 snapshots).

	Total	Meta*	Other**	Relevant	
fr	**728,266**	25,244	369,948	337,074	**46%**
en	**905,963**	46,202	667,430	192,331	**21%**
de	**88,912**	7,235	49,672	32,005	**36%**
pl	**110,369**	4,975	95,241	10,153	**9%**
zh	**131,752**	8,195	112,520	1,037	**0.7%**

* templates definitions, help pages, user talks, etc.
** other languages, redirection links, etc.

Table 1: Ratio of "relevant" articles in wiktionaries

By "relevant", we mean an article about a word in the wiktionary's own language (e.g. not an article about a French word in the English Wiktionary). Among the "relevant" articles, some are empty and some do not contain any translation nor synonym link. Therefore, before deciding to use Wiktionary, it is necessary to compare the amount of extracted information contribution and the amount of work required to obtain it .

3 Study of synonymy networks

In this section, we study synonymy networks built from different resources. First, we introduce some general properties of lexical networks (§3.1). Then we explain how we build Wiktionary's synonymy network and how we analyse its properties. In §3.3, we show how we build similar graphs from traditional resources for evaluation purposes.

3.1 Structure of lexical networks

In the following sections, a graph $G = (V, E)$ is defined by a set V of n vertices and a set $E \subset V^2$ of m edges. In this paper, V is

[4] http://it.wiktionary.org/w/index.php?title=cardinale&oldid=758205

[5] http://en.wiktionary.org/wiki/WT:ELE

[6] http://meta.wikimedia.org/wiki/List_of_Wiktionaries

a set of words and E is defined by a relation $E \overset{R}{\longmapsto} E : (w_1, w_2) \in E$ if and only if $w_1 \overset{R}{\to} w_2$.

Most of lexical networks, as networks extracted from real world, are small worlds (SW) networks. Comparing structural characteristics of wiktionary-based lexical networks to some standard resource should be done according to well-known properties of SW networks (Watts and Strogatz, 1998; Barabasi et al., 2000; Newman, 2003; Gaume et al., 2008). These properties are:

• **Edge sparsity:** SW are sparse in edges $m = O(n)$ or $m = O(n\, log(n))$

• **Short paths:** in SW, the average path length (L)[7] is short. Generally there is at least one short path between any two nodes.

• **High clustering:** in SW, the clustering coefficient (C) that expresses the probability that two distinct nodes adjacent to a given third one are adjacent, is an order of magnitude higher than for Erdos-Renyi (random) graphs: $C_{SW} \gg C_{random}$; this indicates that the graph is locally dense, although it is globally sparse.

• **Heavy-tailed degree distribution:** the distribution of the vertices incidence degrees follows a power law in a SW graph. The probability $P(k)$ that a given node has k neighbours decreases as a power law, $P(k) \approx k^a$ (a being a constant characteristic of the graph). Random graphs conforms to a Poisson Law.

3.2 Wiktionary's network

Graph extraction Considering what said in §2.2.2 and §2.4, we made the following choices:[8]

• **Vertices:** a vertex is built for each entry's part of speech.

• **Parts of speech:** when modeling the links from X (X having for part of speech Pos_X) to one of its synonyms Y, we assume that $Pos_Y = Pos_X$, thus building vertex Pos_Y`.Y`.

• **Subsenses:** subsenses are flattened. First, the subsenses are not always mentioned in the synonyms section. Second, if we take into account the subsenses, they only appear in the source of the relation. For example, considering in figure 1 the relation *boot* $\xrightarrow{syn}$ *kick* (both nouns), and given the 10 subsenses for *boot* and the 5 ones for *kick*, we should build 15 vertices. And we should then add all the links between the mentioned *boot*'s subsenses and the 5 *kick*'s existing subsenses. This would lead to a high number of edges, but the graph would not be closer to the reality. The way subsenses appear in Wiktionary are unpredictable. "Subsenses" correspond sometimes to homonyms or clear-cut senses of polysemous words, but can also correspond to facets, word usage or regular polysemy. Moreover, some entries have no subsenses distinction whereas it would be worthy. More globally, the relevance of discrete word senses has been seriously questioned, see (Victorri and Fuchs, 1996) or (Kilgarriff, 1997) for very convincing discussions. Two more practical reasons led us to this choice. We want our method to be reproducible for other languages and some wiktionaries do not include subsenses. At last, some gold standard resources (eg. Dicosyn) have their subsenses flattened too and we want to compare the resources against each other.

• **Edges:** wiktionary's synonymy links are oriented but we made the graph symmetric. For example, *boot* does not appear in *kick*'s synonyms. Some words even appear as synonyms without being an entry of Wiktionary.
From the *boot* example (figure 1), we extract vertices {`N.boot`, `V.boot`}, build {`N.buskin`, `N.kick`, `V.kick`} and we add the following (symmetrized) edges: `N.boot`↔`N.buskin`, `N.boot`↔`N.kick` and `V.boot`↔`V.kick`.

Graph properties By observing the table 2, we can see that the graphs of synonyms extracted from Wiktionary are all typical small worlds. Indeed their l_{lcc} remains short, their C_{lcc} is always greater or equal than 0.2 and their distribution curves of the vertices incidence degree is very close to a power law (a least-square method gives always exponent $a_{lcc} \approx -2.35$ with a confidence r^2_{lcc} always greater than 0.89). It can also be seen that the average incidence k_{lcc} ranges from 2.32 to 3.32.[9] It means that no matter which language

[7]Average length of the shortest path between any two nodes.

[8]These choices can clearly be discussed from a linguistic point of view and judged to be biased. Nevertheless, we adopted them as a first approximation to make the modelling possible.

[9]It is noteworthy that the mean incidence of vertices is almost always the same (close to 2.8) no matter the graph size is. If we assume that all wiktionary's graphs grow in a similar way but at different speed rates (after all it is the same framework), graphs (at least their statistical properties) from different languages can be seen as snapshots of the same graph at different times. This would mean that the number of graphs edges tends to grow proportionally with the number of vertices. This fits with the dynamic properties of small worlds (Steyvers and Tenenbaum, 2005). It means that for a wiktionary system, even with many contributions, graph density is likely to remain constant and we will see that in comparison to traditional lexical resources this density is quite low.

graph	n	m	n_{lcc}	m_{lcc}	k_{lcc}	l_{lcc}	C_{lcc}	a_{lcc}	r^2_{lcc}
fr-N	18017	9650	3945	4690	2.38	10.18	0.2	-2.03	0.89
fr-A	5411	2516	1160	1499	2.58	8.86	0.23	-2.04	0.95
fr-V	3897	1792	886	1104	2.49	9.84	0.21	-1.65	0.91
en-N	22075	11545	3863	4817	2.49	9.7	0.24	-2.31	0.95
en-A	8437	4178	2486	3276	2.64	8.26	0.2	-2.35	0.95
en-V	6368	3274	2093	2665	2.55	8.33	0.2	-2.01	0.93
de-N	32824	26622	12955	18521	2.86	7.99	0.28	-2.16	0.93
de-A	5856	6591	3690	5911	3.2	6.78	0.24	-1.93	0.9
de-V	5469	7838	4574	7594	3.32	5.75	0.23	-1.92	0.9
pl-N	8941	4333	2575	3143	2.44	9.85	0.24	-2.31	0.95
pl-A	1449	731	449	523	2.33	7.79	0.21	-1.71	0.94
pl-V	1315	848	601	698	2.32	5.34	0.2	-1.61	0.92

n: number of vertices — m: number of edges
k: avg. number of neighbours per vertex — l: avg. path length between vertices
C: clustering rate — a: power law exponent with r^2 confidence
$_{lcc}$: denotes on *largest connected component*

Table 2: Wiktionary synonymy graphs properties

or part of speech, $m = O(n)$ as for most of SW graphs (Newman, 2003; Gaume et al., 2008).

3.3 Building synonymy networks from known standards

WordNet There are many possible ways for building lexical networks from PWN. We tried several methods but only two of them are worth to be mentioned here. The graphs we built have words as vertices, not synsets or senses. A first straightforward method (method A) consists in adding an edge between two vertices only if the corresponding words appear as elements of the same synset. This method produced many disconnected graphs of various sizes. Both the computational method we planned to use and our intuitions about such graphs were pointing towards a bigger graph that would cover most of the lexical network.

We therefore decided to exploit the hypernymy relation. Traditional dictionaries indeed propose hypernyms when one look for synonyms of very specific terms, making hypernymy the closest relation to synonymy at least from a lexicographic viewpoint. However, adding all the hypernymy relations resulted in a network extremely dense in edges with some vertices having a high number of neighbours. This was due to the tree-like organisation of WordNet that gives a very special importance to higher nodes of the tree.

In the end we retained method B that consists in adding edges in following cases:

- if two words belong to the same synset;
- if a word only appears in a synset that is a leaf of the tree and contains only this word, then create edges linking to words included in the hypernym(s) synset.

Therefore when a vertice w do not get any neighbour according to method A, method B adds edges linking w to words included in the hypernym(s) synset of the synset $\{w\}$. We only added hypernyms for the leaves of the tree in order to keep our relations close to the synonymy idea. This idea has already been exploited for some WordNet-based semantic distances calculation taking into account the depth of the relation in the tree (Leacock and Chodorow, 1998).

Dicosyn graphs Dicosyn is a compilation of synonym relations extracted from seven dictionaries (Bailly, Benac, Du Chazaud, Guizot, Lafaye, Larousse and Robert):[10] there is an edge $r \rightarrow s$ if and only if r and s have the same syntactic category and at least one dictionary proposes s being a synonym in the dictionary entry r. Then, each of the three graphs (Nouns, Verbs, Adjectives) obtained is made symmetric (*dicosyn-fr-N, dicosyn-fr-V and dicosyn-fr-A*).

Properties of the graphs extracted Table 3 sums-up the structural properties of the synonyms networks built from standard resources.

We can see that all the synonymy graphs extracted from PWN or Dicosyn are SW graphs. Indeed their l_{lcc} remains short, their C_{lcc} is always greater or equal than 0.35 and their distribution curves of the vertices incidence degree is very close to a power law (a least-square method gives always exponent a_{lcc} near of -2.30 with a confidence r^2_{lcc} always greater than 0.85). It can also be observed that no matter the part of speech, the average incidence of Dicosyn-based graphs is always lower than WordNet ones.

We would like to study the evolution through time of wiktionaries, however this is outside the scope of this paper.

[10]Dicosyn has been first produced at ATILF, before being corrected at CRISCO laboratory. (http://elsap1.unicaen.fr/dicosyn.html)

graph	n	m	n_{lcc}	m_{lcc}	k_{lcc}	l_{lcc}	C_{lcc}	a_{lcc}	r^2_{lcc}
pwn-en-N-A	117798	104929	12617	28608	4.53	9.89	0.76	-2.62	0.89
pwn-en-N-B	117798	168704	40359	95439	4.73	7.79	0.72	-2.41	0.91
pwn-en-A-A	21479	22164	4406	11276	5.12	9.08	0.75	-2.32	0.85
pwn-en-A-B	21479	46614	15945	43925	5.51	6.23	0.78	-2.09	0.9
pwn-en-V-A	11529	23019	6534	20806	6.37	5.93	0.7	-2.34	0.87
pwn-en-V-B	11529	40919	9674	39459	8.16	4.66	0.64	-2.06	0.91
dicosyn-fr-N	29372	100759	26143	98627	7.55	5.37	0.35	-2.17	0.92
dicosyn-fr-A	9452	42403	8451	41753	9.88	4.7	0.37	-1.92	0.92
dicosyn-fr-V	9147	51423	8993	51333	11.42	4.2	0.41	-1.88	0.91

Table 3: Gold standard's synonymy graphs properties

4 Wiktionary graphs evaluation

Coverage and global SW analysis By comparing tables 2 and 3, one can observe that:

• The lexical coverage of Wiktionary-based synonyms graphs is always quantitatively lower than those of standard resources although this may change. For example, *to horn* (in PWN), absent from Wiktionary in 2008, appeared in 2009. At last, Wiktionary is more inclined to include some class of words such as *to poo* (childish) or *to prefetch, to google* (technical neologisms).

• The average number of synonyms for an entry of a Wiktionary-based resource is smaller than those of standard resources. For example, common synonyms such as *to act/to play* appear in PWN and not in Wiktionary. Nevertheless, some other appear (rightly) in Wiktionary: *to reduce/to decrease, to cook/to microwave.*

• The clustering rate of Wiktionary-based graphs is always smaller than those of standard resources. This is particularly the case for English. However, this specificity might be due to differences between the resources themselves (Dicosyn vs. PWN) rather than structural differences at the linguistic level.

Evaluation of synonymy In order to evaluate the quality of extracted synonymy graphs from Wiktionary, we use recall and precision measure. The objects we compare are not simple sets but graphs ($G = (V; E)$), thus we should compare separately set of vertices (V) and set of edges (E). Vertices are words and edges are synonymy links. Vertices evaluation leads to measure the resource coverage whereas edges evaluation leads to measure the quality of the synonymy links in Wiktionary resource.

First of all, the global picture (table 4) shows clearly that the lexical coverage is rather poor. A lot of words included in standard resources are not included yet in the corresponding wiktionary resources. Overall the lexical coverage is always lower than 50%. This has to be kept in mind while looking at the evaluation of relations shown in table 5. To compute the relations evaluation, each resource has been first restricted to the links between words being present in each resource.

About PWN, since every link added with method A will also be added with method B, the precision of Wiktionary-based graphs synonyms links will be always lower for "method A graphs" than for "method B graphs". Precision is rather good while recall is very low. That means that a lot of synonymy links of the standard resources are missing within Wiktionary. As for Dicosyn, the picture is similar with even better precision but very low recall.

5 Exploiting Wiktionary for improving Wiktionary

As seen in section 4, Wiktionary-based resources are very incomplete with regard to synonymy. We propose two tasks for adding some of these links:

Task 1: Adding synonyms to Wiktionary by taking into account its Small World characteristics for proposing new synonyms.

(a) English Wiktionary vs. Wordnet

	Precision	Recall
Nouns	$14120/22075 = 0.64$	$14120/117798 = 0.12$
Adj.	$5874/8437 = 0.70$	$5874/21479 = 0.27$
Verbs	$5157/6368 = 0.81$	$5157/11529 = 0.45$

(b) French Wiktionary vs. Dicosyn

	Precision	Recall
Nouns	$10393/18017 = 0.58$	$10393/29372 = 0.35$
Adj.	$3076/5411 = 0.57$	$3076/9452 = 0.33$
Verbs	$2966/3897 = 0.76$	$2966/9147 = 0.32$

Table 4: Wiktionary coverage

(a) English wiktionary vs. Wordnet

	Precision	Recall
Nouns (A)	$2503/6453 = 0.39$	$2503/11021 = 0.23$
Nouns (B)	$2763/6453 = 0.43$	$2763/18440 = 0.15$
Adj. (A)	$786/3139 = 0.25$	$786/5712 = 0.14$
Adj. (B)	$1314/3139 = 0.42$	$1314/12792 = 0.10$
Verbs (A)	$866/2667 = 0.32$	$866/10332 = 0.08$
Verbs (B)	$993/2667 = 0.37$	$993/18725 = 0.05$

(b) French wiktionary vs. Dicosyn

	Precision	Recall
Nouns	$3510/5075 = 0.69$	$3510/44501 = 0.08$
Adj.	$1300/1677 = 0.78$	$1300/17404 = 0.07$
Verbs	$899/1267 = 0.71$	$899/23968 = 0.04$

Table 5: Wiktionary synonymy links precision & recall

Task 2: Adding synonyms to Wiktionary by taking into account the translation relations.
We evaluate these two tasks against the benchmarks presented in section 3.2.

5.1 Improving synonymy in Wiktionary by exploiting its small world structure

We propose here to enrich synonymy links of Wiktionary by taking into account that lexical networks have a high clustering coefficient. Our hypothesis is that missing links in Wiktionary should be within clusters.

A high clustering coefficient means that two words which are connected to a third one are likely to be connected together. In other words neighbours of my neighbours should also be in my neighbourhood. We propose to reverse this property to the following hypothesis: "neighbour of my neighbours which are not in my neighbourhood should be a good neighbour candidate". Thus the first method we test consist simply in connecting every vertex to neighbours of its neighbours. One can repeat this operation until the expected number of edges is obtained.[11]

Secondly we used the PROX approach proposed by (Gaume et al., 2009). It is a stochastic method designed for studying "Hierarchical Small Worlds". Briefly put, for a given vertex u, one computes for all other vertices v the probability that a randomly wandering particle starting from u stands in v after a fixed number of steps. Let $P(u, v)$ be this value. We propose to connect u to the k first vertices ranked in descending order with respect of $P(u, v)$. We always choose k proportionally to the original degree of u (number of neighbours of u).

For a small number of steps (3 in our case) random wanderings tend to be trapped into local cluster structures. So a vertex v with a high $P(u, v)$ is likely to belong to the same cluster as u, which means that a link u↔v might be relevant.

Figure 2 shows precision, recall and f-score evolution for French verbs graph when edges are added using "neighourhood" method (neigh), and using "Prox" method. Dashed line correspond to the value theoretically obtained by choosing edges at random. First, both methods are clearly more efficient than a random addition, which is not surprising but it seems to confirm our hypothesis that missing edges are within clusters. Adding sharply

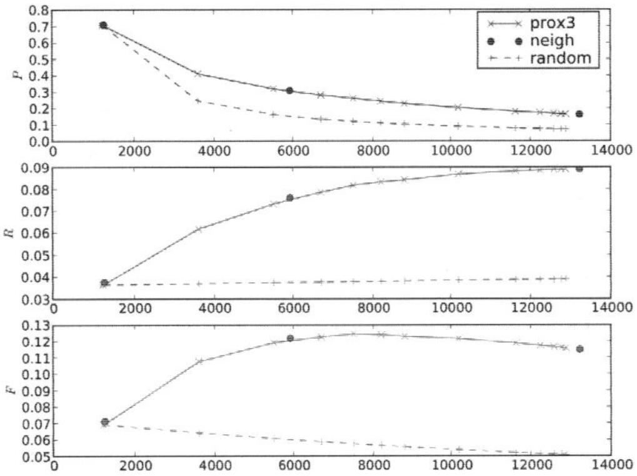

Figure 2: Precision, recall and F-score of French verbs graph enlarged using only existing synonymy links

neighbours of neighbours seems to be as good as adding edges ranked by Prox, anyway the rank provided by Prox permits to add a given number of edges. This ranking can also be useful to order potential links if one think about a user validation system. Synonyms added by Prox and absent from gold standards are not necessarily false.
For example Prox proposes a relevant link *absolve/forgive*, not included in PWN. Moreover, many false positive are still interesting to consider for improving the resource. For example, Prox adds relations such as hypernyms (*to uncover/to peel*) or inter-domain 'synonyms' (*to skin/to peel*). This is due to high clustering (see §3.1) and to the fact that clusters in synonymy networks correlates with language concepts (Gaume et al., 2008; Duvignau and Gaume, 2008; Gaume et al., 2009; Fellbaum, 1999).

Finally note that results are similar for other parts of speech and other languages.

5.2 Using Wiktionary's translation links to improve its synonymy network

Assuming that two words sharing many translations in different languages are likely to be synonymous, we propose to use Wiktionary's translation links to enhance the synonymy network of a given language.

In order to rank links to be potentially added, we use a simple Jaccard measure: let T_w be the set of a word w's translations, then for every couple of words (w, w') we have:

$$Jaccard(w, w') = \frac{|T_w \cap T_{w'}|}{|T_w \cup T_{w'}|}$$

We compute this measure for every possible pair of words and then, starting from Wiktionary's synonymy graph, we incrementally add links according to their Jaccard rank.

[11] We repeat it only two times, otherwise the number of added edges is too large.

We notice first that most of synonymy links added by this method were not initially included in Wiktionary's synonymy network. For example, regarding English verbs, 95% of 2000 best ranked proposed links are new. Hence this method may be efficient to improve graph density. However one can wonder about the quality of the new added links, so we discuss precision in the next paragraph.

In figure 3 is depicted the evolution of precision, recall and F-score for French verbs in the enlarged graph in regard of the total number of edges. We use Dicosyn graph as a gold standard. The dashed line corresponds to theoretical scores one can expect by adding randomly chosen links.

First we notice that both precision and recall are significantly higher than we can expect from random addition. This confirms that words sharing the same translations are good synonym candidates. Added links seem to be particularly relevant at the beginning for higher Jaccard scores. From the first dot to the second one we add about 1000 edges (whereas the original graph contains 1792 edges) and the precision only decreases from 0.71 to 0.69.

The methods we proposed in this section are quite simple and there is room for improvement. First, both methods can be combined in order to improve the resource using translation links and then using clusters structure. One can also think to the corollary task that would consists in adding translation links between two languages using synonymy links of others languages.

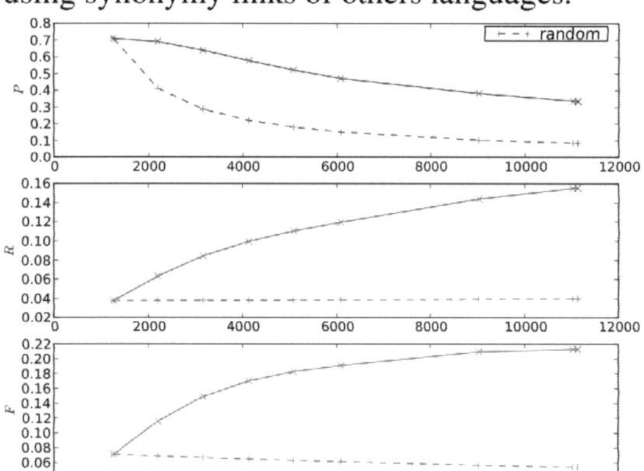

Figure 3: Precision, recall and F-score of French verbs graph enlarged using translation links

6 Conclusion and future work

This paper gave us the opportunity to share some Wiktionary experience related lexical resources building. We presented in addition two approaches for improving these resources and their evaluation. The first approach relies on the small world structure of synonymy networks. We postulated that many missing links in Wiktionary should be added among members of the same cluster. The second approach assumes that two words sharing many translations in different languages are likely to be synonymous. The comparison with traditional resources shows that our hypotheses are confirmed. We now plan to combine both approaches.

The work presented in this paper combines a NLP contribution involving data extraction and rough processing of the data and a mathematical contribution concerning graph-like resource. In our viewpoint the second aspect of our work is therefore complementary of other NLP contributions, like (Zesch et al., 2008b), involving more sophisticated NLP processing of the resource.

Support for collaborative editing Our results should be useful for setting up a more efficient framework for Wiktionary collaborative editing. We should be able to always propose a set of synonymy relations that are likely to be. For example, when a contributor creates or edits an article, he may think about adding very few links but might not bother providing an exhaustive list of synonyms. Our tool can propose a list of potential synonyms, ordered by relevancy. Each item of this list would only need to be validated (or not).

Diachronic study An interesting topic for future work is a "diachronic" study of the resource. It is possible to access Wiktionary at several stages, this can be used for studying how such resources evolve. Grounded on this kind of study, one may predict the evolution of newer wiktionaries and foresee contributors' NLP needs. We would like to set up a framework for everyone to test out new methodologies for enriching and using Wiktionary resources. Such observatory, would allow to follow not only the evolution of Wiktionary but also of Wiktionary-grounded resources, that will only improve thanks to steady collaborative development.

Invariants and variabality Wiktionary as a massively mutiligual synonymy networks is an extremely promising resource for studying the (in)variability of semantic pairings such as *house/family, child/fruit, feel/know...* (Sweetser, 1991; Gaume et al., 2009). A systematic study within the semantic approximation framework presented in the paper on Wiktionary data will be carried on in the future.

References

A-L. Barabasi, R. Albert, H. Jeong, and G. Bianconi. 2000. Power-Law Distribution of the World Wide Web. *Science*, 287. (in Technical Comments).

M. Baroni, F. Chantree, A. Kilgarriff, and S. Sharoff. 2008. Cleaneval: a Competition for Cleaning Web Pages. In *Proceedings of the Conference on Language Resources and Evaluation (LREC)*, Marrakech.

Encyclopaedia Britannica. 2006. Fatally flawed: refuting the recent study on encyclopedic accuracy by the journal Nature.

K. Duvignau and B. Gaume. 2008. Between words and world: Verbal "metaphor" as semantic or pragmatic approximation? In *Proceedings of International Conference "Language, Communication and Cognition"*, Brighton.

C. Fellbaum, editor. 1998. *WordNet: An Electronic Lexical Database*. MIT Press.

C. Fellbaum. 1999. La représentation des verbes dans le réseau sémantique Wordnet. *Langages*, 33(136):27–40.

B. Gaume, K. Duvignau, L. Prévot, and Y. Desalle. 2008. Toward a cognitive organization for electronic dictionaries, the case for semantic proxemy. In *Coling 2008: Proceedings of the Workshop on Cognitive Aspects of the Lexicon (COGALEX 2008)*, pages 86–93, Manchester.

B. Gaume, K. Duvignau, and M. Vanhove. 2009. Semantic associations and confluences in paradigmatic networks. In M. Vanhove, editor, *From Polysemy to Semantic Change: Towards a Typology of Lexical Semantic Associations*, pages 233–264. John Benjamins Publishing.

J. Giles. 2005. Internet encyclopaedias go head to head. *Nature*, 438:900–901.

C. Jacquin, E. Desmontils, and L. Monceaux. 2002. French EuroWordNet Lexical Database Improvements. In *Proceedings of the Third International Conference on Intelligent Text Processing and Computational Linguistics (CICLING 2002)*, Mexico City.

F. Keller and M. Lapata. 2002. Using the web to overcome data sparseness. In *Proceedings of EMNLP-02*, pages 230–237.

A. Kilgarriff and G. Grefenstette. 2003. Introduction to the special issue on the web as corpus. *Computational Linguistics*, 29:333–347.

A. Kilgarriff. 1997. I don't believe in word senses. *Computers and the humanities*, 31(2):91–113.

C. Leacock and M. Chodorow. 1998. Combining local context and wordnet similarity for word sense identification. In C. Fellbaum, editor, *WordNet: An electronic lexical database*, pages 265–283. MIT Press.

M. Newman. 2003. The structure and function of complex networks.

B. Sagot and D. Fišer. 2008. Building a Free French Wordnet from Multilingual Resources. In *Proceedings of OntoLex 2008*, Marrackech.

M. Steyvers and J. B. Tenenbaum. 2005. The large-scale structure of semantic networks: Statistical analyses and a model of semantic growth. *Cognitive Science*, 29:41–78.

E. Sweetser. 1991. *From etymology to pragmatics*. Cambridge University Press.

D. Tufis. 2000. Balkanet design and development of a multilingual balkan wordnet. *Romanian Journal of Information Science and Technology*, 7(1-2).

B. Victorri and C. Fuchs. 1996. *La polysémie, construction dynamique du sens*. Hermès.

D.J. Watts and S.H. Strogatz. 1998. Collective dynamics of small-world networks. *Nature*, 393:440–442.

T. Zesch, C. Müller, and I. Gurevych. 2008a. Extracting Lexical Semantic Knowledge from Wikipedia and Wiktionary. In *Proceedings of the Conference on Language Resources and Evaluation (LREC)*, Marrakech.

T. Zesch, C. Muller, and I. Gurevych. 2008b. Using wiktionary for computing semantic relatedness. In *Proceedings of 23rd AAAI Conference on Artificial Intelligence*.

Using the Wiktionary Graph Structure for Synonym Detection

Timothy Weale, Chris Brew, Eric Fosler-Lussier
Department of Computer Science and Engineering
The Ohio State University
{weale,cbrew,fosler}@cse.ohio-state.edu

Abstract

This paper presents our work on using the graph structure of Wiktionary for synonym detection. We implement semantic relatedness metrics using both a direct measure of information flow on the graph and a comparison of the list of vertices found to be "close" to a given vertex. Our algorithms, evaluated on ESL 50, TOEFL 80 and RDWP 300 data sets, perform better than or comparable to existing semantic relatedness measures.

1 Introduction

The recent creation of large-scale, collaboratively constructed semantic resources provides researchers with cheap, easily accessible information. Previous metrics used for synonym detection had to be built using co-occurrence statistics of collected corpora (Higgins, 2004) or expensive, expert-created resources such as WordNet or Roget's Thesaurus (Jarmasz and Szpakowicz, 2003). Here, we evaluate the effectiveness of Wiktionary, a collaboratively constructed resource, as a source of semantic relatedness information for the synonym detection problem.

Researching these metrics is important because they have been empirically shown to improve performance in a variety of NLP applications, including word sense disambiguation (Turdakov and Velikhov, 2008), real-world spelling errors (Budanitsky and Hirst, 2006) and coreference resolution (Strube and Ponzetto, 2006).

Synonym detection is a recognized testbed for comparing semantic relatedness metrics (e.g (Zesch et al., 2008)). In this task, a target word or phrase is presented to the system, which is then presented with four alternative words or phrases. The goal of the system is to pick the alternative most related to the target. Example questions can be found in Figure 1.

Through the Wikimedia Foundation,[1] volunteers have created two large-scale, collaborative resources that have been used in previous relatedness research – Wikipedia (an encyclopedia) and Wiktionary (a dictionary). These sources have been used for synonym detection and replicating human relatedness evaluations using the category structure (Strube and Ponzetto, 2006), local link structure (Milne and Witten, 2008) and (Turdakov and Velikhov, 2008) and global features (Zesch et al., 2008). They contain related information but focus on different information needs; which information source provides better results depends on the needs of the task. We use Wiktionary which, due to its role as a dictionary, focuses on common words and definitions – the type of information found in our synonym detection problems.

Both Wikipedia and Wiktionary are organized around a basic "page" unit, containing information about an individual word, phrase or entity in the world – definitions, thesaurus entries, pronunciation guides and translations in Wiktionary and general biographical, organizational or philosophical information in Wikipedia. In both data sets, pages are linked to each each other and to a user-created category structure – a graph structure where pages are vertices of the graph and page links are the graph edges. We will leverage this graph for determining relatedness.

[1] http://www.wikimedia.org/

Source Word	Alternative Words
make	earn, print, trade, borrow
flawed	imperfect, tiny, lustrous, crude
solitary	alone, alert, restless, fearless

Figure 1: Example TOEFL Questions

Proceedings of the 2009 Workshop on the People's Web Meets NLP, ACL-IJCNLP 2009, pages 28–31,
Suntec, Singapore, 7 August 2009. ©2009 ACL and AFNLP

2 Extracting Relatedness Measures

We define relatedness based on information flow through the entire Wiktionary graph, rather than by any local in-bound or out-bound link structure. This provides a global measurement of vertex importance, as we do not limit the approach to comparing immediate neighbors.

To do this, we first run the PageRank algorithm (Brin and Page, 1998) iteratively over the graph until convergence to measure the a priori importance of each vertex in graph:

$$\vec{PR}_{t+1} = \alpha \times \left(\vec{PR}_t \cdot E\right) + (1-\alpha) \times \vec{J} \quad (1)$$

In this, E contains the edge transition probabilities, set to a uniform out-bound probability. $\vec{PR}$ holds the PageRank value for each vertex and $\vec{J}$ is uniform vector used to randomly transition between vertices. Traditionally, $\alpha = 0.85$ and is used to tradeoff between a strict transition model and the random-walk model.

We then adopt the extensions proposed in (Ollivier and Senellart, 2007) (**OS**) to determine relatedness given a source vertex:

$$\vec{R}_{t+1} = \alpha \times \left(\vec{R}_t \cdot E + (\vec{S} - \vec{PR})\right) + (1-\alpha) \times \vec{J} \quad (2)$$

$\vec{S}$ is a vector that contains zeros except for a one at our source vertex, and $\vec{PR}$ removes an overall value of 1 based on the a priori PageRank value of the vertex. In this way, vertices close to the source are rewarded with weight and vertices that have a high a priori importance are penalized. When $\vec{R}$ converges, it contains measures of importance for vertices based on the source vertex.

Final relatedness values are then calculated from the vector generated by Equation 2 and the a priori importance of the vector based on the PageRank from Equation 1:

$$rel_{OS}(w, a) = \vec{R}_w[a] \times \log\left(\frac{1}{PR[a]}\right) \quad (3)$$

w is the vertex for the source word and a is the alternative word vertex. The $PR[a]$ penalty is used to further ensure that our alternative vertex is not highly valued simply because it is well-connected.

Applying Equation 3 provides comparable semantic relatedness performance (see Tables 1 and 2). However, cases exist where a single data value is insufficient to make an adequate determination of word relatedness because of small differences for candidate words. We can incorporate additional relatedness information about our vertices by leveraging information about the set of vertices deemed "most related" to our current vertex.

2.1 Integrating N-Best Neighbors

We add information by looking at the similarity between the n-best related words for each vertex. Intuitively, given a source word w and candidate alternatives a_1 and a_2,[2] we look at the set of words that are semantically related to each of the candidates (represented as vectors W, A_1 and A_2). If the overlap between elements of W and A_1 is greater than W and A_2, A_1 is more likely to be the synonym of W.

Highly-ranked shared elements are good indicators of relatedness and should contribute more than low-ranked related words. Lists with many low-ranked words could be an artifact of the data set and should not be ranked higher than ones containing a few high-ranked words.

Our ranked-list comparison metric (**NB**) is a selective mean reciprocal ranking function:

$$rel_{NB}(\vec{W}, \vec{A}, n) = \sum_{r=1}^{n} \frac{1}{r} \times \delta(W_r \in \vec{A}) \quad (4)$$

$\vec{W}$ is the n-best list based on the source vertex and $\vec{A}$ is the n-best list based on the alternative vertex. Values are added to our relatedness metric based on the position of a vertex in the target list and the traditional Dirac δ-function, which has a value of one if the target vertex appears anywhere in our candidate list and a zero in all other cases.

Each metric (OS and NB) will have different ranges. We therefore normalize the reported value by scaling each based on the maximum value for that portion in order to achieve a uniform scale.

Our final metric (**OS+NB**) is created by averaging the two normalized scores. In this work, both scores are given equal weighting. Deriving weightings for combining the two scores will be part of our future work.

$$rel_{OS+NB}(w_{i,j}) = \frac{OS(c_i, c_j) + NB(c_i, c_j, n)}{2} \quad (5)$$

In this, $OS()$ returns the normalized $rel_{OS}()$ value and $NB()$ returns the normalized rel_{NB} value. The maximum $rel_{P+N}()$ value of 1.0 is achieved if c_j has the highest PageRank-based value and the highest N-Best value.

[2] See Figure 1

Source	*ESL* Acc. (%)	*TOEFL* Acc. (%)
JPL	82	78.8
LC-IR	78	81.3
OS	86	88.8
NB	80	88.8
OS+NB	88	93.8

Table 1: ESL and TOEFL Performance

3 Evaluation

We present performance results on three data sets. The first, ESL, uses 50 questions from the English as a Second Language test (Turney, 2001). Next, an 80 question data set from the Test of English as a Foreign Language (TOEFL) is used (Landauer and Dumais, 1997). Finally, we evaluate on the Reader's Digest WordPower (RDWP) data set (Jarmasz and Szpakowicz, 2003). This is a set of 300 synonym detection problems gathered from the Word Power game of the Canadian edition of Reader's Digest Word from 2000 – 2001.

We use the Feb. 03, 2009 version of the English Wiktionary data set [3] for extracting graph structure and relatedness information.

Table 1 presents the performance of our algorithm on the ESL and TOEFL test sets. Our results are compared to Jarmasz and Szpakowicz (2003), which uses a path-based cost on the structure of Roget's Thesaurus (**JPL**) and a cooccurence-based metric, **LC-IR** (Higgins, 2004), which constrained context to only consider adjacent words in structured web queries.

Information about our algorithm's performance on the RDWP test set is found in Table 2. Our results are compared to the previously mentioned algorithms and also the work of Zesch et al. (2008). Their first metric (**ZPL**) uses the path length between two graph vertices for relatedness determination. The second, (**ZCV**), creates concept vectors based on a distribution of pages that contain a particular word.

RDWP is not only larger then the previous two, but also more complictated. TOEFL and ESL average 1.0 and 1.008 number of words in each source and alternative, respectively. For RDWP each entry averages 1.4 words.

We map words and phrases to graph vertices by first matching against the page title. If there is no match, we follow the approach outlined in (Zesch et al., 2008). Common words are removed from the phrase[4] and for every remaining word in the phrase, we determine the page mapping for that individual word. The relatedness of the phrase is then set to be the maximum relatedness value attributed to any of the individual words in the phrase.

Random guessing by an algorithm could increase algorithm performance through random chance. Therefore, we present both a overall percentage and also a precision-based percentage. The first (*Raw*) is defined as the correct number of guesses over all questions. The second (*Prec*) is defined as the correct number of guesses divided by only those questions that were attempted.

3.1 Discussion

For NB and OS+NB, we set $n = 3000$ based on TOEFL data set training.[5] Testing was then performed on the ESL and RDWP data set.

As shown in Table 1, the OS algorithm performs better on the task than the comparison systems. On its own, NB relatedness performs well – at or slightly worse than OS. Combining the two measures increases performance on both data sets. While our TOEFL results are below the reported performance of (Turney et al., 2003) (97.5%), we do not use any task-dependent learning for our results and our algorithms have better performance than any individual module in their system.

Combining OS with NB mitigates the influence of OS when it is not confident. OS correctly picks '*pinnacle*' as a synonym of '*zenith*' with a relatedness value 126,000 times larger than its next competitor. For '*consumed*', OS is wrong, giving '*bred*' a higher score than '*eaten*' – but only by a value 1.2 times that of '*eaten*'. The latter case is overcome by the addition of n-best information while the former is unaffected.

Table 2 demonstrates that we have results comparable to existing state-of-the-art measures. Our choice of n resulted in reduced scores on this task when compared to using the OS metric by itself. But, our algorithm still outperforms both the ZPL and ZCV metrics for our data set in raw scores and in three out of the four precision measures. Further refinement of the RDWP data set mapping or changing our metric score to a weighted sum of

[3] `http://download.wikimedia.org`

[4] Defined here as: {and, or, to, be, the, a, an, of, on, in, for, with, by, into, is, no}

[5] Out of 1.1 million vertices

Metric	Source	Attempted	Score	# Ties	Raw	Prec
JPL	Roget's	300	223	0	.74	.74
LC-IR	Web	300	224.33	-	.75	.75
ZPL	Wikipedia	226	88.33	96	.29	.39
ZCV		288	165.83	2	.55	.58
ZPL	Wiktionary	201	103.7	55	.35	.52
ZCV		174	147.3	3	.49	.85
OS	Wiktionary	300	234	0	.78	.78
NB		300	212	0	.71	.71
OS+NB		300	227	0	.76	.76

Table 2: Reader's Digest WordPower 300 Overall Performance

sorts (rather than a raw maximum) could result in increased performance.

Wiktionary's coverage enables all words in the first two tasks to be found (with the exception of 'bipartisanly'). Enough of the words in the RDWP task are found to enable the algorithm to attempt all synonym detection questions.

4 Conclusion and Future Work

In this paper, we have demonstrated the effectiveness of Wiktionary as a source of relatedness information when coupled with metrics based on information flow using synonym detection as our evaluation testbed.

Our immediate work will be in learning weights for the combination measure, using (Turney et al., 2003) as our guideline. Additional work will be in automatically determining an effective value for n across all data sets.

Long-term work will be in modifying the page transition values to achieve non-uniform transition values. Links are of differing quality, and the transition probabilities should reflect that.

References

Sergey Brin and Lawrence Page. 1998. The Anatomy of a Large-Scale Hypertextual Web Search Engine. *Computer Networks and ISDN Systems*, 30(1–7):107–117.

Alexander Budanitsky and Graeme Hirst. 2006. Evaluating WordNet-based Measures of Lexical Semantic Relatedness. *Computational Linguistics*, 32(1):13–47.

Derrick Higgins. 2004. Which Statistics Reflect Semantics? Rethinking Synonymy and Word Similarity. In *Proceedings of the International Conference on Linguistic Evidence*.

Mario Jarmasz and Stan Szpakowicz. 2003. Roget's Thesaurus and Semantic Similarity. In *Proceedings of Conference on Recent Advances in Natural Language Processing (RANLP 2003)*.

Thomas K. Landauer and Susan T. Dumais. 1997. A Solution to Plato's Problem: The Latent Semantic Analysis Theory of Acquisition, Induction, and Representation of Knowledge. *Psychological Review*.

David Milne and Ian H. Witten. 2008. An Effective, Low-Cost Measure of Semantic Relatedness Obtained from Wikipedia Links. In *Proceedings of AAAI 2008*.

Yann Ollivier and Pierre Senellart. 2007. Finding Related Pages Using Green Measures: An Illustration with Wikipedia. In *Proceedings of AAAI 2007*.

Michael Strube and Simone Paolo Ponzetto. 2006. WikiRelate! Computing Semantic Relatedness Using Wikipedia. In *AAAI*.

Denis Turdakov and Pavel Velikhov. 2008. Semantic relatedness metric for Wikipedia concepts based on link analysis and its application to word sense disambiguation. In *Proceedings of CEUR*.

Peter D. Turney, Michael L. Littman, Jeffrey Bigham, and Victor Shnayder. 2003. Combining Independent Modules in Lexical Multiple-Choice Problems. In *Recent Advances in Natural Language Processing III: Selected Papers from RANLP 2003*.

Peter D. Turney. 2001. Mining the Web for Synonyms: PMI-IR versus LSA on TOEFL. In *Proceedings of the Twelfth European Conference on Machine Learning (ECML-2001)*, pages 491–502, Freidburg, Germany.

Torsten Zesch, Christof Muller, and Iryna Gurevych. 2008. Using Wiktionary for Computing Semantic Relatedness. In *Proceedings of AAAI 2008*.

Automatic Content-based Categorization of Wikipedia Articles

Zeno Gantner
University of Hildesheim
Machine Learning Lab
gantner@ismll.de

Lars Schmidt-Thieme
University of Hildesheim
Machine Learning Lab
schmidt-thieme@ismll.de

Abstract

Wikipedia's article contents and its category hierarchy are widely used to produce semantic resources which improve performance on tasks like text classification and keyword extraction. The reverse – using text classification methods for predicting the categories of Wikipedia articles – has attracted less attention so far. We propose to "return the favor" and use text classifiers to improve Wikipedia. This could support the emergence of a virtuous circle between the *wisdom of the crowds* and machine learning/NLP methods.

We define the categorization of Wikipedia articles as a multi-label classification task, describe two solutions to the task, and perform experiments that show that our approach is feasible despite the high number of labels.

1 Introduction

Wikipedia's article contents and its category hierarchy are widely used to produce semantic resources which improve performance on tasks like text classification and keyword extraction (Banerjee, 2007; Gabrilovich and Markovitch, 2007; Minier et al., 2007; Mihalcea and Csomai, 2007; Wang and Domeniconi, 2008; Medelyan et al., 2008). The reverse – using text classification methods to improve Wikipedia's article-category mappings – has attracted less attention (Fu et al., 2007).

A system that automatically suggests categories for Wikipedia articles will help to improve the encyclopedia for its users and authors, as well as the semantic resources created from it.

The complexity of Wikipedia's category systems[1] and sheer number of categories make it hard for – possibly inexperienced – authors to assign categories to new or existing articles. As of February 2009, the German Wikipedia has about 886,000 articles, which belong to about 64,000 categories. For the English Wikipedia, those numbers are even higher.[2]

Classical document classification data sets like Reuters RCV1-V2 (Lewis et al., 2004) have around 100 different categories. In comparison, the automatic categorization of Wikipedia articles is a challenging task, as it involves tens to hundreds of thousand categories. For such large-scale classification problems, particular attention is necessary to deal with both training and prediction complexity, as well as imbalanced class distributions.

In this article, we present the problem of content-based article categorization in Wikipedia, and suggest an evaluation protocol as well as two content-based methods for solving this problem.

2 Problem Statement

Let $X \subseteq \mathcal{X}$ be the set of all articles and L be the set of all category labels in one of Wikipedia's language versions. Each article $x \in X$ is assigned a set of $k(x)$ category labels $\{l_1, \ldots, l_{k(x)}\} \subseteq L$.

In this context, one can think of several prediction problems: Given an article x without category information, predict all the article's categories. This scenario is typical for newly created articles, thus we call it the **new article problem**. Another prediction task would be to predict the missing categories for an article with existing, but incomplete category information (**missing categories problem**). Such a condition can occur e.g. if a new category is created and the creator of the new category does not include all existing articles that should be assigned to that category. In this pa-

[1] We use the plural here, as each language version has its own category hierarchy. The categories may be linked across languages using so-called interlanguage links.

[2] http://stats.wikimedia.org/

Proceedings of the 2009 Workshop on the People's Web Meets NLP, ACL-IJCNLP 2009, pages 32–37,
Suntec, Singapore, 7 August 2009. ©2009 ACL and AFNLP

		$f_i(x)$	
		1	-1
$\hat{f}_i(x)$	1	tp_i	fp_i
	-1	fn_i	tn_i

Table 1: Confusion matrix for class i.

per, we will concentrate on the *new article problem*.

Such a problem is a so-called *multi-label*, or *any-of* classification task, as opposed to *single-label* (*one-of*) classification (Manning et al., 2008). Multi-label classification can be expressed as a set of binary classification problems:

$$f(x) = \{l_i | f_i(x) = 1\}, \quad (1)$$

where $f_i : \mathcal{X} \rightarrow \{-1, 1\}, 1 \leq i \leq |L|$ are indicator functions for class l_i, i.e. $f_i(x) = 1$ iff. article x is annotated with the category label l_i.

The associated learning problem is to find a prediction model $\hat{f}$ that predicts categories for given articles as good as possible, according to a given loss function.

We choose micro- and macro-averaged F_1 as loss functions. Micro-averaged F_1 is computed from the complete confusion matrix, while macro-averaged F_1 is the average F_1 computed from class-wise confusion matrices. Micro-averaged measures tend to measure the effectiveness of a classifier on the large categories, while macro-averaging gives more weight to smaller categories (Manning et al., 2008).

$$F_1^{\text{macro}} := \frac{1}{|L|} \sum_{i=1}^{|L|} \frac{2 \cdot \text{tp}_i}{2 \cdot \text{tp}_i + \text{fp}_i + \text{fn}_i}, \quad (2)$$

where tp_i is the number of true positives, fp_i the number of false positives, and fn_i the number of false negatives for class i (see Table 1).

$$F_1^{\text{micro}} := \frac{2 \cdot \text{tp}}{2 \cdot \text{tp} + \text{fp} + \text{fn}}, \quad (3)$$

where $\text{tp} = \sum_{i=1}^{|L|} \text{tp}_i$ is the overall number of true positives, $\text{fp} = \sum_{i=1}^{|L|} \text{fp}_i$ the overall number of false positives, and $\text{fn} = \sum_{i=1}^{|L|} \text{fn}_i$ the overall number of false negatives.

F_1 is widely used in information retrieval and supervised learning tasks. While providing a balance between precision and recall, optimizing for F_1 "forces" the prediction method and the respective learning algorithm to decide which category labels to predict and which ones not – just predicting a ranking of labels is not sufficient. This is motivated by the intended use of the prediction method in a category suggestion system for Wikipedia articles: Such a system cannot present an arbitrarily high number of (possibly ranked) suggestions to the user, who would be overwhelmed by the amount of information. On the other hand, if there is a fixed low number of suggestions, there would be the danger of correct category labels being left out.

3 Methods

There are many multi-label classification models in the literature, which are either adaptions of existing single-label models, or models generated by transformation of the multi-label problem to single-label problems, which are then solved using again existing single-label models. Tsoumakas et al. (2009) give an overview of multi-label classification methods.

Wikipedia articles are hypertext pages. For classifying hypertext pages, there are two obvious kinds of features: (i), there are *content-based features*, like words or n-grams contained in the articles, and (ii), there are *link-based features*, such as in- and outgoing article links, links to external web pages, and the (estimated or actually known) categories of the linked articles. Past research on relational learning and hypertext classification (Lu and Getoor, 2003) has shown that both kinds of features are useful, and that the strongest methods combine both. It makes sense to investigate content-based features as well as link-based features, because improvements in any of the two can lead to overall improvements. The work presented here focuses on content-based features.

A naive approach would be to directly take the binary representation of multi-label classification (equation 1), and then to train binary classifier models like support-vector machines (SVM, Cortes and Vapnik (1995)):

$$\hat{f}_{\text{naive}}(x) := \{l_i | \hat{f}_i(x) = 1\} \quad (4)$$

As the training of a traditional binary SVM classifier does not optimize towards the given multi-label loss function, but for accuracy, we do not expect the best results from this method.

If we want better multi-label predictions, changing the threshold of the binary decision functions is a straightforward solution. We employed two well-known thresholding strategies, ranking cut (RCut) and score cut (SCut, Yang (2001)), to predict Wikipedia categories.

RCut sorts all labels according to their binary prediction score $\hat{f}_i^*$, and selects the t top labels:

$$\hat{f}_{\text{rcut}}(x) := \text{argmax}^t_{1 \le i \le |L|} \hat{f}_i^*(x), \tag{5}$$

where $\text{argmax}^t_{a \in A}\, g(a)$ refers to the t elements of A with highest value $g(a)$. The value of the hyper-parameter threshold t can be chosen empirically on a hold-out set.

SCut uses an individual decision threshold s_i for each label:

$$\hat{f}_{\text{scut}}(x) := \{l_i | \hat{f}_i^*(x) \ge s_i\} \tag{6}$$

Good threshold values s_i can be determined during training. Algorithm 1 shows a category-wise optimization of the threshold values as described by Yang (2001). Because it tunes the threshold s_i for each category based on the F_1 measure over that category, it optimizes for macro-averaged F_1. If we are able to find optimal thresholds for each category, then we will achieve optimal macro-F_1 performance, as the following lemma says.

Lemma 1 *Let*

$$s_i := \mathit{argmax}_{s \in S}\, F_1(X, Y_i, \hat{f}_i), \tag{7}$$

$$\hat{f}_i(x) := \begin{cases} 1, & \mathit{if}\ \hat{f}_i^*(x) > s \\ -1, & \mathit{otherwise} \end{cases} \tag{8}$$

Then

$$(s_1, ..., s_{|L|}) = \mathit{argmax}_{(s'_1, ..., s'_{|L|})} F_1^{\mathit{macro}}(X, Y, \hat{f}), \tag{9}$$

$$\hat{f}(x) := \{l_i | \hat{f}_i^*(x) > s'_i\}) \tag{10}$$

i.e., the component-wise binary F_1 optimization yields the F_1^{macro}-optimal multi-label threshold.

Proof: The components of the sum in the definition of macro-averaged F_1 (Equation 2) are exactly the class-wise F_1 values. The choice of s_i influences only the part of the sum $\frac{2 \cdot \text{tp}_i}{2 \cdot \text{tp}_i + \text{fp}_i + \text{fn}_i}$ belonging to i. Thus each s_i can be optimized independently.

Representing each category label as binary prediction problem, as in the work presented here, requires $|L|$ binary classifiers. There also exist methods that use $|L|^2$ binary classifiers (Mencia and Fürnkranz, 2008), which is not feasible if L is large.

Algorithm 1 Macro-averaged F_1 optimization for SCut

Input: binary classifiers $(\hat{f}_i^*)$, $\hat{f}_i^* : \mathcal{X} \to S$; training instances $X \subseteq \mathcal{X}$ and labels $Y \in \mathcal{P}(L)^{|X|}$
Output: thresholds (s_i)

```
for i = 1 to |L| do
    Y_i ← binary labels for category i generated from Y
    s_i ← argmax_{s∈S} F1-measure for f̂_i* with threshold s on X, Y_i
end for
return (s_i)
```

4 Experiments

To demonstrate the general feasibility of the automatic categorization of Wikipedia articles, we conducted experiments on a subset of the German Wikipedia. In this section, we describe the extracted data sets, the evaluation protocol, and discuss the results.

4.1 Category Data

To generate the data set for the experiment, we used the official database dumps of the German Wikipedia, generated December 6, 2008.[3] We then extracted all articles belonging to the category *Eishockey* ("ice-hockey") or to one of its descendants, and removed all category labels from outside the chosen category sub-graph, and all category labels of categories containing less than 5 articles. We proceeded identically for the category *Philosoph* ("philosopher").

Feature generation was performed as follows: First, we removed all wiki markup from the article source code. Second, we used Mallet (McCallum, 2002) to generate bag-of-words representations of the articles. All tokens were converted to lower case, and tokens occurring in only one article were removed. We conducted no stopword removal, nor stemming. Finally, we normalized the feature vectors to sum up to one.

Table 2 shows some properties of the data. $|X|$ is the number of instances, $|L|$ the number of distinct category labels; the fourth column contains the number of features (words) in the data set.[4]

[3] `http://download.wikimedia.org`

[4] The data can be downloaded from `http://www.domain/path`.

top category	$\|X\|$	$\|L\|$	# features
Philosoph	2,445	55	68,541
Eishockey	5,037	159	36,473

Table 2: Data set properties.

4.2 Evaluation Protocol

Train-Test Split

For the experiment, we randomly separated the data sets into 80% of the articles for training, and 20% for testing. To evaluate the *new article problem*, we removed all category labels from the articles in the test sets.

Training

As an experimental baseline, we used a static classifier (*most-frequent*) that always predicts the most frequent categories, regardless of the article.

We implemented the RCut and SCut strategies using linear support-vector machines from the LIBSVM library (Chang and Lin, 2001) for the underlying binary classification task. For each category, we used 5-fold cross-validation to find a good value for the hyperparameter C (Hsu et al., 2003). As SVMs perform only binary decisions, but do not yield scores suitable for ranking the labels, we used LIBSVM's modified version of Platt's method (Platt, 2000) to obtain probabilities, which are used as scores for the RCut rankings and the SCut decisions. As SCut's threshold search goes over an infinite set $S = [0, 1]$ (Algorithm 1, line 3), we did an approximate search over this interval with step size 0.01. For RCut and *most-frequent*, we report results for all thresholds $1, \ldots, |L|$. In an application setting, we would have to determine a suitable t using a hold-out data set.

4.3 Results and Discussion

The results can be seen in Table 3 and Figure 1 and 2. Both methods clearly perform better than the baseline. For macro-averaged F_1 on *Eishockey*, SCut performs better than RCut, which is not surprising, as this method is optimized towards macro-averaged F_1. For *Philosoph*, RCut with a rank threshold of $t = 3$ has a little bit (by 0.005) higher macro-averaged F_1 result, but this is likely not a significant difference.

The experiments show that simple models like the transformation from multi-label to binary problems, combined with thresholding strategies like SCut and RCut, are suitable for the categorization of Wikipedia articles: The methods achieve a good prediction quality, while the number of underlying binary classifiers scales linearly (see Section 3).

5 Conclusion and Future Work

In this article, we view the categorization of Wikipedia articles as a multi-label classification problem and report experiments on a subset of the German Wikipedia. The experiments show that there are suitable models for the categorization of Wikipedia articles.

We propose to use machine learning algorithms in order to improve the category assignments of Wikipedia articles. While data from Wikipedia is already widely used to improve text classification systems, it may be desirable to "return the favor" and use text classifiers to improve Wikipedia. This could support the emergence of a virtuous circle between the wisdom of the crowds and machine "intelligence", i.e. machine learning and NLP methods.

Wikipedia category data could be used as well for generating publicly available, large-scale (hierarchical) multi-label classification benchmark collections with different characteristics. Furthermore, it could provide the basis for multilingual document classification data sets.

To be able to provide category suggestions for large Wikipedias like the German, the Spanish or the English one, we will extend our experiments to larger subsets, and finally to all of the German and English Wikipedia. In order to achieve this, we will also investigate hierarchical multi-label classification methods (Liu et al., 2005; Cai and Hofmann, 2004; Cesa-Bianchi et al., 2006) and faster training algorithms for linear SVMs and logistic regression (Fan et al., 2008; Shalev-Shwartz et al., 2007). Given that we use $|L|$ binary classifiers for our models, this should be feasible, even for large numbers of categories. It would also be interesting to compare our methods to the work by Fu et al. (2007), which concentrates on link-based categorization of Wikipedia articles.

Other promising research directions are the examination of Wikipedia-specific features, and the survey of large-scale multi-label classification algorithms that take into account dependencies between labels.

	micro-averaged			macro-averaged		
	P	R	F_1	P	R	F_1
method	*Philosoph*					
most-frequent ($t = 1$)	0.489	0.315	0.383	0.009	0.019	0.012
most-frequent ($t = 55$)	0.028	1.0	0.055	0.028	1.0	0.049
RCut ($t = 2$)	0.522	0.674	0.589	0.252	0.283	0.244
RCut ($t = 3$)	0.395	0.764	0.520	0.240	0.379	0.266
SCut	0.341	0.735	0.466	0.225	0.350	0.261
method	*Eishockey*					
most-frequent ($t = 2$)	0.214	0.162	0.185	0.001	0.007	0.003
most-frequent ($t = 159$)	0.008	1.0	0.016	0.008	1.0	0.017
RCut ($t = 1$)	0.829	0.628	0.715	0.499	0.472	0.494
RCut ($t = 2$)	0.526	0.796	0.633	0.406	0.599	0.497
SCut	0.646	0.806	0.717	0.461	0.630	0.554

Table 3: Results for data sets *Philosoph* and *Eishockey*.

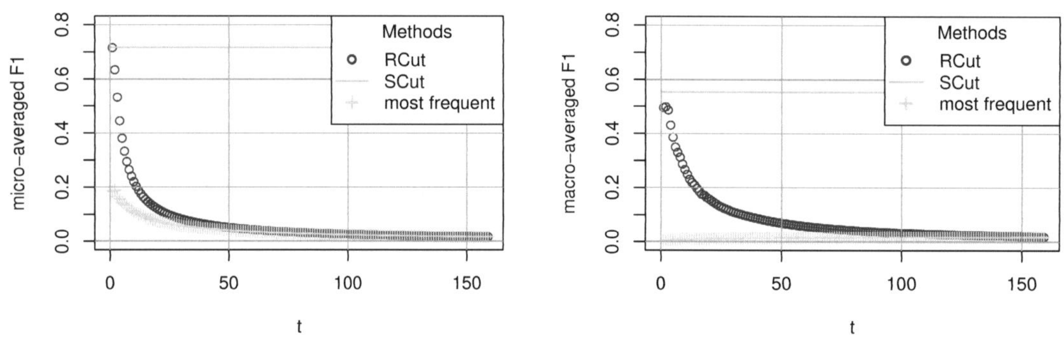

Figure 1: Method comparison for F_1 on data set *Eishockey*. SCut does not depend on t.

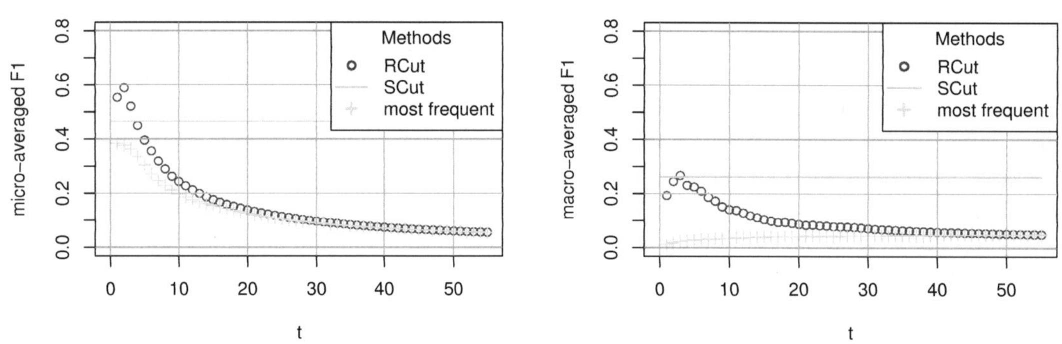

Figure 2: Method comparison for F1 on data set *Philosoph*. SCut does not depend on t.

Acknowledgments

The authors gratefully acknowledge the partial co-funding of their work through the European Commission FP7 project MyMedia (www.mymediaproject.org) under the grant agreement no. 215006.

References

Somnath Banerjee. 2007. Boosting inductive transfer for text classification using Wikipedia. In *ICMLA '07: Proceedings of the Sixth International Conference on Machine Learning and Applications*, Washington, DC, USA. IEEE Computer Society.

Lijuan Cai and Thomas Hofmann. 2004. Hierarchical document categorization with support vector machines. In *Proceedings of the 13th ACM International Conference on Information and Knowledge Management (CIKM '04), November 8-13, 2004, Washington, D.C., USA*. ACM Press, New York, NY, USA.

Nicol Cesa-Bianchi, Claudio Gentile, and Luca Zaniboni. 2006. Incremental algorithms for hierarchical classification. *Journal of Machine Learning Research*.

Chih-Chung Chang and Chih-Jen Lin, 2001. *LIBSVM: a library for support vector machines*. Software available at `http://www.csie.ntu.edu.tw/~cjlin/libsvm`.

Corinna Cortes and Vladimir Vapnik. 1995. Support–vector networks. *Machine Learning*, 20.

Rong-En Fan, Kai-Wei Chang, Cho-Jui Hsieh, Xiang-Rui Wang, and Chih-Jen Lin. 2008. Liblinear: A library for large linear classification. *Journal of Machine Learning Research*, 9.

Linyun Fu, Haofen Wang, Haiping Zhu, Huajie Zhang, Yang Wang, and Yong Yu. 2007. Making more Wikipedians: Facilitating semantics reuse for wikipedia authoring. In *ISWC/ASWC 2007*.

Evgeniy Gabrilovich and Shaul Markovitch. 2007. Harnessing the expertise of 70,000 human editors: Knowledge-based feature generation for text categorization. *Journal of Machine Learning Research*.

Chih-Wei Hsu, Chih-Chung Chang, and Chih-Jen Lin. 2003. A practical guide to support vector classification. Technical report, Department of Computer Science, National Taiwan University.

David D. Lewis, Yiming Yang, Tony G. Rose, G. Dietterich, Fan Li, and Fan Li. 2004. RCV1: A new benchmark collection for text categorization research. *Journal of Machine Learning Research*.

Tie-Yan Liu, Yiming Yang, Hao Wan, Hua-Jun Zeng, Zheng Chen, and Wei-Ying Ma. 2005. Support vector machines classification with a very large-scale taxonomy. *SIGKDD Explorations*, (1).

Qing Lu and Lise Getoor. 2003. Link-based classification using labeled and unlabeled data. In *ICML Workshop on "The Continuum from Labeled to Unlabeled Data in Machine Learning and Data Mining"*.

Christopher D. Manning, Prabhakar Raghavan, and Hinrich Schütze. 2008. *Introduction to Information Retrieval*. Cambridge University Press, New York.

Andrew Kachites McCallum. 2002. Mallet: A machine learning for language toolkit. http://mallet.cs.umass.edu.

Olena Medelyan, Ian H. Witten, and David Milne. 2008. Topic indexing with Wikipedia. In *Proceedings of the Wikipedia and AI workshop at AAAI-08*. AAAI.

Eneldo Loza Mencia and Johannes Fürnkranz. 2008. Efficient pairwise multilabel classification for large-scale problems in the legal domain. In Walter Daelemans, Bart Goethals, and Katharina Morik, editors, *ECML/PKDD (2)*, volume 5212 of *Lecture Notes in Computer Science*, pages 50–65. Springer.

Rada Mihalcea and Andras Csomai. 2007. Wikify!: linking documents to encyclopedic knowledge. In *CIKM '07*, New York, NY, USA. ACM.

Zsolt Minier, Zalan Bodo, and Lehel Csato. 2007. Wikipedia-based kernels for text categorization. In *SYNASC '07*, Washington, DC, USA. IEEE Computer Society.

J. Platt. 2000. Probabilistic outputs for support vector machines and comparison to regularized likelihood methods. In *Advances in Large Margin Classifiers*.

S. Shalev-Shwartz, Y. Singer, and N. Srebro. 2007. Pegasos: Primal estimated sub–gradient solver for SVM. In *Proceedings of the International Conference on Machine Learning*.

G. Tsoumakas, I. Katakis, and I. Vlahavas. 2009. Mining multi-label data. unpublished book chapter.

Pu Wang and Carlotta Domeniconi. 2008. Building semantic kernels for text classification using Wikipedia. In *KDD '08*, New York, NY, USA. ACM.

Yiming Yang. 2001. A study on thresholding strategies for text categorization. In W. Bruce Croft, David J. Harper, Donald H. Kraft, and Justin Zobel, editors, *SIGIR 2001*, pages 137–145. ACM.

Evaluating a Statistical CCG Parser on Wikipedia

Matthew Honnibal **Joel Nothman** **James R. Curran**
School of Information Technologies
University of Sydney
NSW 2006, Australia
{mhonn, joel, james}@it.usyd.edu.au

Abstract

The vast majority of parser evaluation is conducted on the 1984 Wall Street Journal (WSJ). In-domain evaluation of this kind is important for system development, but gives little indication about how the parser will perform on many practical problems.

Wikipedia is an interesting domain for parsing that has so far been under-explored. We present statistical parsing results that for the first time provide information about what sort of performance a user parsing Wikipedia text can expect.

We find that the C&C parser's standard model is 4.3% less accurate on Wikipedia text, but that a simple self-training exercise reduces the gap to 3.8%. The self-training also speeds up the parser on newswire text by 20%.

1 Introduction

Modern statistical parsers are able to retrieve accurate syntactic analyses for sentences that closely match the domain of the parser's training data. Breaking this domain dependence is now one of the main challenges for increasing the industrial viability of statistical parsers. Substantial progress has been made in adapting parsers from newswire domains to scientific domains, especially for biomedical literature (Nivre et al., 2007). However, there is also substantial interest in parsing encyclopedia text, particularly Wikipedia.

Wikipedia has become an influential resource for NLP for many reasons. In addition to its variety of interesting metadata, it is massive, constantly updated, and multilingual. Wikipedia is now given its own submission keyword in general CL conferences, and there are workshops largely centred around exploiting it and other collaborative semantic resources.

Despite this interest, there have been few investigations into how accurately existing NLP processing tools work on Wikipedia text. If it is found that Wikipedia text poses new challenges for our processing tools, then our results will constitute a baseline for future development. On the other hand, if we find that models trained on newswire text perform well, we will have discovered another interesting way Wikipedia text can be exploited.

This paper presents the first evaluation of a statistical parser on Wikipedia text. The only previous published results we are aware of were described by Ytrestøl et al. (2009), who ran the LinGo HPSG parser over Wikipedia, and found that the correct parse was in the top 500 returned parses for 60% of sentences. This is an interesting result, but one that gives little indication of how well a user could expect a parser to actually annotate Wikipedia text, or how to go about adjusting one if its performance is inadequate.

To investigate this, we randomly selected 200 sentences from Wikipedia, and hand-labelled them with CCG annotation in order to evaluate the C&C parser (Clark and Curran, 2007). C&C is the fastest deep-grammar parser, making it a likely choice for parsing Wikipedia, given its size.

Even at the parser's WSJ speeds, it would take about 18 days to parse the current English Wikipedia on a single CPU. We find that the parser is 54% slower on Wikipedia text, so parsing a full dump is inconvenient at best. The parser is only 4.3% less accurate, however.

We then examine how these figures might be improved. We try a simple domain adaptation experiment, using self-training. One of our experiments, which involves self-training using the Simple English Wikipedia, improves the accuracy of the parser's standard model on Wikipedia by 0.8%. The bootstrapping also makes the parser faster. Parse speeds on newswire text improve 20%, and speeds on Wikipedia improve by 34%.

Proceedings of the 2009 Workshop on the People's Web Meets NLP, ACL-IJCNLP 2009, pages 38–41,
Suntec, Singapore, 7 August 2009.

Corpus	Sentences	Mean length
WSJ 02-21	39,607	23.5
FEW	889,027 (586,724)	22.4 (16.6)
SEW	224,251 (187,321)	16.5 (14.1)

Table 1: Sentence lengths before (and after) length filter.

2 CCG Parsing

Combinatory Categorial Grammar (CCG) (Steedman, 2000) is a linguistically motivated grammar formalism with several advantages for NLP. Like HPSG, LFG and LTAG, a CCG parse recovers the semantic structure of a sentence, including long-range dependencies and complement/adjunct distinctions, providing substantially more information than skeletal brackets.

Clark and Curran (2007) describe how a fast and accurate CCG parser can be trained from CCGbank (Hockenmaier and Steedman, 2007). One of the keys to the system's success is *supertagging* (Bangalore and Joshi, 1999). Supertagging is the assignment of lexical categories before parsing. The parser is given only tags assigned a high probability, greatly restricting the search space it must explore. We use this system, referred to as C&C, for our parsing experiments.

3 Processing Wikipedia Data

We began by processing all articles from the March 2009 dump of Simple English Wikipedia (SEW) and the matching Full English Wikipedia (FEW) articles. SEW is an online encyclopedia written in basic English. It has stylistic guidelines that instruct contributors to use basic vocabulary and syntax, to improve the articles' readability. This might make SEW text easier to parse, making it useful for our self-training experiments.

`mwlib` (PediaPress, 2007) was used to parse the MediaWiki markup. We did not expand templates, and retained only paragraph text tokenized according to the WSJ, after it was split into sentences using the NLTK (Loper and Bird, 2002) implementation of Punkt (Kiss and Strunk, 2006) parameterised on Wikipedia text. Finally, we discarded incorrectly parsed markup and other noise.

We also introduced a sentence length filter for the domain adaptation data (but not the evaluation data), discarding sentences longer than 25 words or shorter than 3 words. The length filter was used to gather sentences that would be easier to parse. The effect of this filter is shown in Table 1.

4 Self-training Methodology

To investigate how the parser could be improved on Wikipedia text, we experimented with semi-supervised learning. We chose a simple method, self-training. Unlabelled data is annotated by the system, and the predictions are taken as truth and integrated into the training system.

Steedman et al. (2003) showed that the selection of sentences for semi-supervised parsing is very important. There are two issues: the *accuracy* with which the data can be parsed, which determines how noisy the new training data will be; and the *utility* of the examples, which determines how informative the examples will be.

We experimented with a novel source of data to balance these two concerns. Simple English Wikipedia imposes editorial guidelines on the length and syntactic style authors can use. This text should be easier to parse, lowering the noise, but the syntactic restrictions might mean its examples have lower utility for adapting the parser to the full English Wikipedia.

We train the C&C supertagger and parser (Clark and Curran, 2007) on sections 02-21 of the Wall Street Journal (WSJ) marked up with CCG annotations (Hockenmaier and Steedman, 2007) in the standard way. We then parse all of the Simple English Wikipedia remaining after our pre-processing. We discard the 826 sentences the parser could not find an analysis for, and set aside 1,486 randomly selected sentences as a future development set, leaving a corpus of 185,000 automatically parsed sentences (2.6 million words).

We retrain the supertagger on a simple concatenation of the 39,607 WSJ training sentences and the Wikipedia sentences, and then use it with the normal-form derivations and hybrid dependencies model distributed with the parser[1].

We repeated our experiments using text from the full English Wikipedia (FEW) for articles whose names match an article in SEW. We randomly selected a sample of 185,000 sentences from these, to match the size of the SEW corpus.

We also performed a set of experiments where we re-parsed the corpus using the updated supertagger and retrained on output, the logic being that the updated model might make fewer errors, producing higher quality training data. This iterative retraining was found to have no effect.

[1] `http://svn.ask.it.usyd.edu.au/trac/candc`

Model	WSJ Section 23					Wiki 200					Wiki 90k	
	P	R	F	speed	cov	P	R	F	speed	cov	speed	cov
WSJ derivs	85.51	84.62	85.06	545	99.58	81.20	80.51	80.86	394	99.00	239	98.81
SEW derivs	85.06	84.11	84.59	634	99.75	81.96	81.34	81.65	739	99.50	264	99.11
FEW derivs	85.24	84.32	84.78	653	99.79	81.94	81.36	81.65	776	99.50	296	99.15
WSJ hybrid	86.20	84.80	85.50	481	99.58	81.93	80.51	81.22	372	99.00	221	98.81
SEW hybrid	85.80	84.30	85.05	571	99.75	82.16	80.49	81.32	643	99.50	257	99.11
FEW hybrid	85.94	84.46	85.19	577	99.79	82.49	81.03	81.75	665	99.50	275	99.15

Table 2: Parsing results with automatic POS tags. SEW and FEW models incorporate self-training.

5 Annotating the Wikipedia Data

We manually annotated a Full English Wikipedia evaluation set of 200 sentences. The sentences were sampled at random from the 5000 articles that were linked to most often by Wikipedia pages. Articles used for self-training were excluded.

The annotation was conducted by one annotator. First, we parsed the sentences using the C&C parser. We then manually corrected the supertags, supplied them back to the parser, and corrected the parses using a GUI. The interface allowed the annotator to specify bracket constraints until the parser selected the correct analysis. The annotation took about 20 hours in total.

We used the CCGbank manual (Hockenmaier and Steedman, 2005) as the guidelines for our annotation. There were, however, some systematic differences from CCGbank, due to the faulty noun phrase bracketing and complement/adjunct distinctions inherited from the Penn Treebank.

6 Results

The results in this section refer to precision, recall and F-Score over labelled CCG dependencies, which are 5-tuples (head, child, category, slot, range). Speed is reported as words per second, using a single core 2.6 GHz Pentium 4 Xeon.

6.1 Out-of-the-Box Performance

Our experiments were performed using two models provided with v1.02 of the C&C parser. The *derivs* model is calculated using features from the Eisner (1996) normal form derivation. This is the model C&C recommend for general use, because it is simpler and faster to train. The *hybrid* model achieves the best published results for CCG parsing (Clark and Curran, 2007), so we also experimented with this model. The models' performance is shown in the WSJ rows of Table 2. We report accuracy using automatic POS tags, since we did not correct the POS tags in the Wikipedia data.

The derivs and hybrid models show a similar drop in performance on Wikipedia, of about 4.3%. Since this is the first accuracy evaluation conducted on Wikipedia, it is possible that Wikipedia data is simply harder to parse, possibly due to its wider vocabulary. It is also possible that our manual annotation made the task slightly harder, because we did not reproduce the CCGbank noun phrase bracketing and complement/adjunct distinction errors.

We also report the parser's speed and coverage on Wikipedia. Since these results do not require labelled data, we used a sample of 90,000 sentences to obtain more reliable figures. Speeds varied enormously between this sample and the 200 annotated sentences. A length comparison reveals that our manually annotated sentences are slightly shorter, with a mean of 20 tokens per sentence. Shorter sentences are often easier to parse, so this issue may have affected our accuracy results, too.

The 54% drop in speed on Wikipedia text is explained by the way the supertagger and parser are integrated. The supertagger supplies the parser with a beam of categories. If parsing fails, the chart is reinitialised with a wider beam and it tries again. These failures occur more often when the supertagger cannot produce a high quality tag sequence, particularly if the problem is in the tag dictionary, which constrains the supertagger's selections for frequent words. This is why we focused on the supertagger in our domain adaptation experiments.

6.2 Domain Adaptation Experiments

The inclusion of parsed data from Wikipedia articles in the supertagger's training data improves its accuracy on Wikipedia data, with the FEW enhanced model achieving 89.86% accuracy, compared with the original accuracy of 88.77%. The SEW enhanced supertagger achieved 89.45% accuracy. The *derivs* model parser improves in accuracy by 0.8%, the *hybrid* model by 0.5%.

The out-of-domain training data had little impact on the models' accuracy on the WSJ, but did improve parse speed by 20%, as it did on Wikipedia. The speed increases because the supertagger's beam width is decided by its confidence scores, which are more narrowly distributed after the model has been trained with more data.

After self-training, the *derivs* and *hybrid* models performed equally accurately. With no reason to use the hybrid model, the total speed increase is 34%. With our pre-processing, the full Wikipedia dump had close to 1 billion words, so speed is an important factor.

Overall, our simple self-training experiment was quite successful. This result may seem surprising given that the CoNLL 2007 participants generally failed to use similar resources to adapt dependency parsers to biomedical text (Dredze et al., 2007). However, our results confirm Rimell and Clark's (2009) finding that the C&C parser's division of labour between the supertagger and parser make it easier to adapt to new domains.

7 Conclusion

We have presented the first investigation into statistical parsing on Wikipedia data. The parser's accuracy dropped 4.3%, suggesting that the system is still useable out-of-the-box. The parser is also 54% slower on Wikipedia text. Parsing a full Wikipedia dump would therefore take about 52 days of CPU time using our 5-year-old architecture, which is inconvenient, but manageable over multiple processors.

Using simple domain adaptation techniques, we are able to increase the parser's accuracy on Wikipedia, with the fastest model improving in accuracy by 0.8%. This closed the gap in accuracy between the two parser models, removing the need to use the slower *hybrid* model. This allowed us to achieve an overall speed improvement of 34%.

Our results reflect the general trend that NLP systems perform worse on foreign domains (Gildea, 2001). Our results also support Rimell and Clark's (2009) conclusion that because C&C is highly lexicalised, domain adaptation is largely a process of adapting the supertagger.

A particularly promising aspect of these results is that the parse speeds on the Wall Street Journal improved, by 15%. This improvement came with no loss in accuracy, and suggests that further bootstrapping experiments are likely to be successful.

8 Acknowledgements

We would like to thank Stephen Clark and the anonymous reviewers for their helpful feedback. Joel was supported by a Capital Markets CRC PhD scholarship and a University of Sydney Vice-Chancellor's Research Scholarship.

References

Srinivas Bangalore and Aravind Joshi. 1999. Supertagging: An approach to almost parsing. *Computational Linguistics*, 25(2):237–265.

Stephen Clark and James R. Curran. 2007. Wide-coverage efficient statistical parsing with CCG and log-linear models. *Computational Linguistics*, 33(4):493–552.

Mark Dredze, John Blitzer, Partha Pratim Talukdar, Kuzman Ganchev, João Graca, and Fernando Pereira. 2007. Frustratingly hard domain adaptation for dependency parsing. In *Proceedings of the CoNLL Shared Task Session of EMNLP-CoNLL 2007*, pages 1051–1055. ACL, Prague, Czech Republic.

Jason Eisner. 1996. Efficient normal-form parsing for Combinatory Categorial Grammar. In *Proceedings of the Association for Computational Linguistics*, pages 79–86. Santa Cruz, CA, USA.

Daniel Gildea. 2001. Corpus variation and parser performance. In *Proceedings of the EMNLP Conference*, pages 167–202. Pittsburgh, PA.

Julia Hockenmaier and Mark Steedman. 2005. CCGbank manual. Technical Report MS-CIS-05-09, Department of Computer Science, University of Pennsylvania.

Julia Hockenmaier and Mark Steedman. 2007. CCGbank: a corpus of CCG derivations and dependency structures extracted from the Penn Treebank. *Computational Linguistics*, 33(3):355–396.

Tibor Kiss and Jan Strunk. 2006. Unsupervised multilingual sentence boundary detection. *Computational Linguistics*, 32(4):485–525.

Edward Loper and Steven Bird. 2002. NLTK: The natural language toolkit.

Joakim Nivre, Johan Hall, Sandra Kübler, Ryan McDonald, Jens Nilsson, Sebastian Riedel, and Deniz Yuret. 2007. The CoNLL 2007 shared task on dependency parsing. In *Proceedings of the CoNLL Shared Task Session*, pages 915–932. Prague, Czech Republic.

PediaPress. 2007. `mwlib` MediaWiki parsing library. `http://code.pediapress.com`.

Laura Rimell and Stephen Clark. 2009. Porting a lexicalized-grammar parser to the biomedical domain. *Journal of Biomedical Informatics*. (in press).

Mark Steedman. 2000. *The Syntactic Process*. The MIT Press, Cambridge, MA.

Mark Steedman, Rebecca Hwa, Stephen Clark, Miles Osborne, Anoop Sarkar, Julia Hockenmaier, Paul Ruhlen, Steven Baker, and Jeremiah Crim. 2003. Example selection for bootstrapping statistical parsers. In *Proceedings of HLT-NAACL 2003*. Edmonton, Alberta.

Gisle Ytrestøl, Stephan Oepen, and Daniel Flickinger. 2009. Extracting and annotating Wikipedia sub-domains. In *Proceedings of the 7th International Workshop on Treebanks and Linguistic Theories*, pages 185–197. Groningen, Netherlands.

Construction of Disambiguated Folksonomy Ontologies Using Wikipedia

Noriko Tomuro and Andriy Shepitsen
DePaul University, College of Digital Media
243 S. Wabash, Chicago, IL USA
tomuro@cs.depaul.edu, ashepits@cdm.depaul.edu

Abstract

One of the difficulties in using Folksonomies in computational systems is *tag ambiguity*: tags with multiple meanings. This paper presents a novel method for building Folksonomy tag ontologies in which the nodes are disambiguated. Our method utilizes a clustering algorithm called DSCBC, which was originally developed in Natural Language Processing (NLP), to derive *committees* of tags, each of which corresponds to one meaning or domain. In this work, we use Wikipedia as the external knowledge source for the domains of the tags. Using the committees, an ambiguous tag is identified as one which belongs to more than one committee. Then we apply a hierarchical agglomerative clustering algorithm to build an ontology of tags. The nodes in the derived ontology are disambiguated in that an ambiguous tag appears in several nodes in the ontology, each of which corresponds to one meaning of the tag. We evaluate the derived ontology for its *ontological density* (how close similar tags are placed), and its usefulness in applications, in particular for a personalized tag retrieval task. The results showed marked improvements over other approaches.

1 Introduction

In recent years, there has been a rapid growth in social tagging systems – so-called *Folksonomies* where users assign keywords or tags to categorize resources. Typically, the sources of folksonomies are web resources, and virtually any kind of information available on the Internet, ranging from web pages (e.g. Delicious (delicious.com)), scientific articles (e.g. Bibsonomy (www.bibsonomy.org)) to media resources (e.g. Flickr (www.flickr.com), Last.fm (www.last.fm)). Although tags in folksonomies are essentially semantic concepts, they have distinct characteristics as compared to conventional semantic resources which are often used in Natural Language Processing (NLP), such as WordNet (Miller, 1990). First, folksonomy tags are unrestricted – users are free to choose any words or set of characters to formulate tags. One significant problem arising from such free-formedness is *tag ambiguity*: tags that have several meanings (e.g. "Java" as coffee or a programming language or an island in Indonesia). Second, folksonomy tags are unstructured – tags assigned to a given resource are simply enumerated in a list (although oftentimes using a varying font size to indicate popularity), and no special organization or categorization of the tags is made (by the Folksonomy site). There have been several work recently which extracted structures from folksonomy tags and constructed ontologies (e.g. (Clough et al., 2005), (Schmitz, 2006)). However, most of them evaluate the effect of the extracted structures only in the context of specific applications, for instance generating user recommendations (e.g. (Shepitsen et al., 2008)).

In this work, we develop a novel method for constructing ontologies from folksonomy tags. In particular, we employ a clustering algorithm called *Domain Similarity Clustering By Committee (DSCBC)* (Tomuro et al., 2007). DSCBC is an extension of an algorithm called CBC (Pantel and Lin, 2002), and was originally developed for lexical semantics in NLP to automatically derive single/unambiguous word meanings (as *committees*) from ambiguous words. In this work, DSCBC is effectively adopted to derive disambiguated folksonomy tag committees, where a committee in this context is a cluster of tags in which the members share the same or very similar concept in one of their meanings. By using DSCBC, an ambiguous tag is identified as one which belongs to more than

Proceedings of the 2009 Workshop on the People's Web Meets NLP, ACL-IJCNLP 2009, pages 42–50,
Suntec, Singapore, 7 August 2009. ©2009 ACL and AFNLP

one committee. One of the key ideas in DSCBC is the notion of *feature domain similarity*: the similarity between the features themselves, obtained a priori from sources external to the dataset used at hand. For example, if data instances x and y are represented by features f1 and f2, the feature domain similarity refers to the similarity between f1 and f2 (not between x and y). DSCBC utilizes this feature domain similarity to derive clusters whose domains are 'close', thereby producing unambiguous committees. In this work, we incorporate Wikipedia as the external knowledge resource, and use the similarity between Wikipedia articles to derive the committees of disambiguated tags. Finally using the tag committees derived by DSCBC, we build an ontology of tags by using a modified hierarchical agglomerative clustering algorithm. Ambiguous tags are mapped to several nodes in this ontology.

Note that in this paper, we refer to the structure derived by the hierarchical clustering algorithm as an 'ontology' instead of a 'taxonomy'. That is because, in the algorithm, the parent-child relation is determined by a similarity measure only, therefore sometimes does not correspond to the subsumption relation in the strict sense.

For evaluation, we construct an ontology from the Delicious tags, and measure the quality (*ontological density*) of the derived ontology by comparing with the ontologies obtained without using Wikipedia. We also use the derived ontology in a personalized information retrieval task. The results show that our method achieved marked improvements over other approaches.

2 Related Work

Several efforts have been made recently which focused on extracting structures from folksonomies. Clough (Clough et al., 2005) and Schmitz (Schmitz, 2006) derived hierarchical structures from image folksonomies (St. Andrew collection (specialcollections.st-and.ac.uk/photcol.htm) and Flickr, respectively). In addition to the hierarchical relation, they also derived other relations such as "type of", "aspect of", "same-as", etc. Mika (Mika, 2007) and Heymann (Heymann and Garcia-Molina, 2006) proposed an automatic creation of tags in folksonomy networks based on the tag co-occurrences among resources and users. They then used a graph clustering algorithm to connect tags which were used by the same users and for the same resources to identify tag 'clouds' and communities of like-minded users. However, none of those work used NLP techniques, nor did they deal with the tag ambiguity problem; Oftentimes, highly ambiguous tags are even removed from the data.

In our previous work (Shepitsen et al., 2008), we used a standard hierarchical agglomerative clustering algorithm to build a tag hierarchy. We also considered only the most popular sense of an ambiguous tag and ignored all other senses.

Wikipedia has been attracting much attention in the recent NLP research. For example, Wikipedia as a lexical resource was exploited for thesauri construction (Milne et al., 2006) and for word sense disambiguation (Mihalcea and Csomai, 2007). Other NLP tasks in which Wikipedia was utilized to provide contextual and domain/encyclopedia knowledge include question-answering (Ahn et al., 2004) and information extraction (Culotta et al., 2006). In a similar vein, (Gabrilovich and Markovitch, 2006) also used Wikipedia to improve the accuracy for text categorization. An interesting text retrieval application was done by Gurevych (Gurevych et al., 2007), in which Wikipedia was utilized to improve the retrieval accuracy in matching the professional interests of job applicants with the descriptions of professions/careers.

The work presented in this paper applies an NLP technique (the DSCBC algorithm), which incorporates the domain knowledge (Wikipedia) as a critical component, to the task of extracting semantic structure, in particular an ontology, from folksonomies. Our method is novel, and the experimental results indicate that the derived ontology was of high semantic quality.

3 Deriving Unambiguous Tag Committees

The DSCBC algorithm, which we had developed in our previous work (Tomuro et al., 2007), is an extension of *CBC Clustering* (Pantel and Lin, 2002), modified to produce unambiguous clusters when the data contained ambiguous instances. Assuming the instances are represented by vectors of features/domains, consider the following data:

```
    a b c d
x:  1 1 0 0
y:  1 0 1 0
z:  1 0 0 1
```

where x, y, z are data instances, and a, b, c, d are features. In most clustering algorithms, features are assumed to be independent to each other, or their dependencies are ignored. So in the example, x is equally likely clustered with y or z, because the similarity between x and y, and x and z are the same (based on the Euclidean distance, for example). However if we have a priori, general knowledge about the features that b's domain is more similar to that of c than to d, it is better to cluster x and y instead of x and z, because the $\{x, y\}$ cluster is "tighter" than the $\{x, z\}$ cluster with respect to the domains of the features.

3.1 Feature Domain Similarity

In DSCBC, the general knowledge about the features is incorporated as a measure called *Feature Domain Similarity*: the similarity between the features themselves, obtained a priori from sources external to the dataset used at hand. In this work, we used Wikipedia as the external knowledge source, and as the features to represent the folksonomy tags. To this end, we first obtained the most recent dump of Wikipedia and clustered the articles to reduce the size of the data. We call such a cluster of Wiki articles a *Wiki concept*. Clustering was based on the similarity of the terms which appeared in the articles. Detailed descriptions of the Wikipedia data and this clustering process are given in section 5.1. Then given a set of folksonomy tags T, a set of folksonomy resources R and a set of Wiki concepts W, we defined a matrix M of size $|T| \times |W|$, where the rows are tags and the columns/features are Wiki concepts. Each entry in this matrix, for a tag $t \in T$ and a Wiki concept $w \in W$, was computed as the cosine between two term vectors: one for t where the features are terms used in (all of) the resources in R to which t was assigned (by the folksonomy users), and another for w where the features are terms used in (all of) the Wiki articles in w. Thus, the matrix M contains the similarity values for a given tag to all Wikipedia concepts, thereby identifying the (Wikipedia) domains of the tag.

Using the matrix M, we define the feature domain similarity between two tags f and g, denoted $fdSim(f, g)$, as:

$$fdSim(f,g) = \frac{\sum_i \sum_j f_i \times g_j \times cos(w_i, w_j)}{\sqrt{\sum_i f_i^2 \times \sum_i g_i^2}}$$

where f_i is the similarity of the tag f to the ith Wiki concept (and likewise for g), and $cos(w_i, w_j)$ is the cosine (thus similarity) between the ith and j^{th} Wiki concepts. In this formula, the domain knowledge is incorporated not only through the way a tag is represented (as a vector of Wiki concepts), but also directly by $cos(w_i, w_j)$, the similarity between Wiki concepts themselves.

In addition to Feature Domain Similarity, we also incorporated a measure of *reference tightness* for folksonomy tags and Wiki concepts. This metric measures and takes advantage of the *link structure* in the folksonomy system as well as Wikipedia. For example, when a tag was assigned to several web pages in the folksonomy system, some of those pages may be reachable from each other through hyperlinks – in which case, we can consider the tag's domains are tight. Likewise for Wiki concepts, if a folksonomy tag is 'similar' to several Wiki concepts (for which the similarity value is above some threshold), some of those Wiki concepts may be reachable in the Wikipedia structure – then we can consider the tag's domains are tight as well. Furthermore, based on the notion of reference tightness within a set of resources, we define the connectedness between two sets of resources as the fraction of the resources (web pages or Wiki concepts) in one set which are reachable to resources in another set. We define the reference tightness between two sets of resources S and U, denoted $srt(S, U)$, as follows.

$$srt(S,U) = \frac{\sum_{s \in S, u \in U} reach(s,u) + reach(u,s)}{\sum_{s \in S} nRef(s) + \sum_{u \in U} nRef(u)}$$

where $nRef(k)$ is the number of outgoing reference links in the resource k, and $reach(a, b)$ is an indicator function which returns 1 if any reference link from the resource in a is reachable from any resource in b or 0 otherwise. There are two terms in the numerator because the reachability relation is directional.

3.2 The DSCBC Algorithm

Using the notions of feature domain similarity and reference tightness, we define the similarity between two tags f and g as follows.

$$\begin{aligned} dsSim(f,g) &= \alpha \times fdSim(f,g) \\ &\quad +(1-\alpha) \times srt(R_f, R_g) \end{aligned}$$

where R_f is the set of references from all web pages to which the tag f is assigned, $srt(R_f, R_g)$ is the reference tightness between R_f and R_g, and

α is a weighting coefficient. In our experiments (discussed in section 5), we set α to be 0.8 based on the results of the preliminary runs.

The DSCBC algorithm is shown in Algorithm 1. DSCBC is an unsupervised clustering algorithm which automatically derives a set of *committees*. A committee is a group of folksonomy tags which are very similar to each other. In Phase I, a set of preliminary tag clusters are first created. In Phase II, some of those tag clusters are selected as committees – those which are dissimilar/orthogonal to all other committees selected so far. Then in Phase III, each tag is assigned to committees which are similar to the tag. The $dsSim$ function is used in Phase I and II to measure the similarity between clusters and committees respectively. In Phase III, an ambiguous tag is assigned to one of more committees, where each time the features of the assigned committee are removed from the tag. Thus, ambiguous tags are identified as those which belong to more than one committee.

4 Building Folksonomy Tag Ontology

After obtaining the committees by DSCBC, we organize the tags into a ontology by using a modified hierarchical agglomerative clustering algorithm.[1] We first compute the pair-wise similarity between any two tags and sort those pairs according to the similarity values. Then we take the most similar pair and create the first cluster. Afterwards, we iterate through the whole tag/cluster pairs and substitute all instances in which either tag is a member, if the tag is not ambiguous, by the obtained cluster, and repeat the process until the list of pairs is empty. The committees derived by DSCBC are utilized to identify ambiguous tags – when a tag belonged to more than one committee. When we process an ambiguous tag, we first find its "core meaning" by finding the committee to which the tag is most similar, then remove all (non-zero) features that are encoded in committee from all instances left in the dataset. With this scheme, we can cover all senses of an ambiguous tag, for all such tags, during ontology generation. The similarity is computed using the $dsSim$ function described in the previous section; the only difference that, if one member of a pair is a cluster, it is rep-

[1]Our algorithm is essentially a modification of the Average-Link Clustering by (OConnor and Herlocker, 2001).

Input: Set of tags T. Tuning coefficients:
n - number of the most similar tags chosen for the target tag
q - number of features for finding the centroid
β - similarity threshold for adding tags to committees
γ - similarity threshold for assigning tags to committees
Output: Set of committees C. Set of tags T where each t $\in$ T is assigned to committees in C.
Phase I. Finding set of clusters L
foreach $t_i \in T$ **do**
  Select a set k of n most similar t_j : i $\neq$ j
  add k to L if it is not already in L.
end
Phase II. Find Communities C
foreach $c \in L$ **do**
  Find the centroid of c using only q features shared by most of tags in the cluster
  Add c to C if its similarity to every other cluster is lower than β
end
Phase III. Assign tags to committees
foreach $t \in T$ **do**
  Assign t to committee c in C if the similarity is higher than γ
end
Algorithm 1: Clustering tags using DSCBC

resented by its centroid. Figure 1 shows an example folksonomy ontology. The modified hierarchical agglomerative clustering algorithm is shown in Algorithm 2.

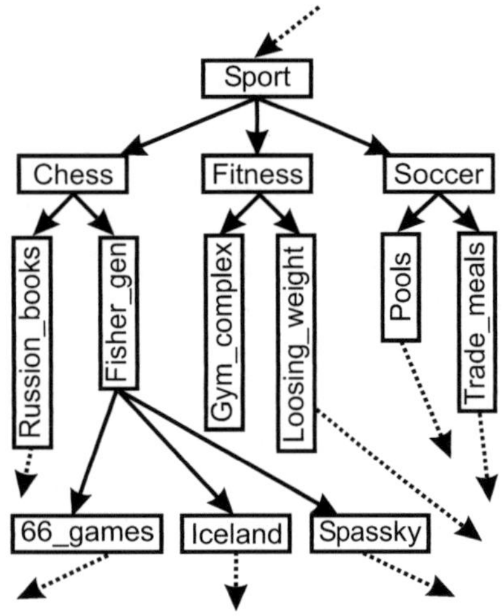

Figure 1: Example Folksonomy Ontology

Input: Set of tags T. Set of Committees C.
Output: An ontology of folksonomy tags.
L is a list containing pairs of tag/clusters with associated similarity, initially empty.
foreach $t_i \in T$ **do**
  Compute the similarity to all other tags t_j (i $\neq$ j), and add a pair $\langle t_i, t_j \rangle$ in L.
end
while *L is not empty* **do**
  1. Sort L by the similarity of the pairs.
  2. Pop the pair with the highest similarity from L. Let it $\langle t_i, \alpha \rangle$. α can be a single tag or a cluster of tags.
  3. Make t_i the parent of α.
  4. Join t_i with α, and create a new cluster β.
  if t_i *belongs to more than one committee in C* **then**
    1. Find the committee c which is the most similar to t_i.
    2. Remove all features intersecting with c from t_i.
  end
  else
    1. Substitute all instances of t_i in the pairs in L by β.
  end
end

Algorithm 2: Ontology Construction Algorithm

5 Experimental Evaluations

We applied our proposed algorithm to data from a real-world social tagging system Delicious and derived a tag ontology. Then we evaluated the derived ontology on two aspects: the *density* of the ontology, and the usefulness of the ontology in a personalized Information Retrieval (IR) task. Note that in the experiments, we determined the values for all tuning coefficients in the algorithms during the preliminary test runs.

5.1 Datasets

We first crawled the Delicious site and obtained data consisting of 29,918 users, 6,403,442 resources and 1,035,177 tags. In this data, 47,184,492 annotations were made by just one user, or for one resource, or by one tag. This distribution followed the Zipf's law – small numbers of tags were in frequent use and large numbers of tags were rarely used. Our intuitions were that the effect of using the semantic/encyclopedia knowledge from Wikipedia would probably be better reflected in the low frequency "long tail" part of the Zipf's distribution rather than the high frequency part. Likewise for users, we have discovered in our previous research that search personalization algorithms often produce different results for users with rich profiles and for users who have sparse profiles. This problem is known as the "Cold Start" problem in search personalization: a new user has very little information/history in the profile, therefore the system cannot reliably infer his/her interests. Since our experiments included a personalized IR task, we decided to extract two subsets from the data: one set containing high frequency tags assigned by users with rich profiles (randomly selected 1,000 most frequent tags entered by 100 high profile users), and another containing low frequency tags assigned by users with sparse profiles (randomly selected 1,000 least frequent tags entered by 100 sparse profile users). We refer to the former set as the "Frequent Set" and the latter set as the "Long Tail Set". The total number of resources in each dataset was 16,635 and 3,356 respectively.

Then for both datasets, we applied a part-of speech tagger to all resources and extracted all nouns (and discarded all other parts of speech). We also applied the Porter Stemmer (tartarus.org/~martin/PorterStemmer) to eliminate terms with inflectional variations. Finally, we represented each resource page as a vector of stemmed terms, and the values were term frequencies.

As for Wikipedia, we used its English version available from BitTorrent Network (www.bittorrent.com). The original data (the most recent dump, as of 24 July, 2008) contained 13,916,311 pages. In order to reduce the size to make the computation feasible, we randomly chose 75,000 pages (which contained at least 50 words) and applied the Maximal Complete Link clustering algorithm to further reduce the size. After clustering, we obtained a total of 43,876 clusters, most of which contained one or two Wiki articles, but some of which had several articles. We call such a Wiki article cluster *Wiki concept*.

As with the tag datasets, for each Wiki article we applied the Porter Stemmer to reduce the number of the terms. Then we represented each Wiki concept page as a vector of stemmed terms, and the values were term frequencies.

5.2 Evaluation 1: Ontological Density

For the first evaluation, we evaluated the derived Delicious tag ontology directly by measuring the topological closeness of similar semantic concepts in the ontology. To that end, we developed a notion of *ontological density*: all tags assigned to a specific resource should be located close to each other in the ontology. For instance, a web resource *java.sun.com* in Delicious is assigned with various tags such as 'Java', 'Programming' and 'Technology'. Those tags should be concentrated in one place rather than scattered over various sections in the ontology. By measuring the distance as the number of edges in the ontology between tags assigned to a specific resource, we can obtain an estimate of the ontology density for the resource. Then finding the average density of all resources can give us an approximation of the overall density of the ontology's quality.

But here a difficulty arises for ambiguous tags – when a tag is ambiguous and located in several places in the ontology. In those cases, we chose the sense (an ontology node) which is the closest to the unambiguous tags assigned to the same resource. For example, Figure 2 shows a part of the ontology where an ambiguous tag 'NLP' (with two senses) is mapped: 1) Natural Language Processing (the left one in the figure), and 2) Neurolinguistic programming (the right one in the figure). The target web resource is tagged with three tags: two unambiguous tags 'POS' and 'Porter', and an ambiguous tag 'NLP'. To identify the sense of 'NLP' for this resource, we count the number of edges from the two unambiguous tags ('POS', 'Porter') to both 'NLP' tag nodes, and select the one which has the shortest distance. In the figure, the first sense has the total distance of 4 (= 2 edges from 'Pos' + 2 edges from 'Porter'), while the second sense has the distance 10 (= 5 edges from 'Pos' + 5 edges from 'Porter'). Therefore, we select the first sense ('Natural Language Processing') as the meaning of 'NLP' for this resource.

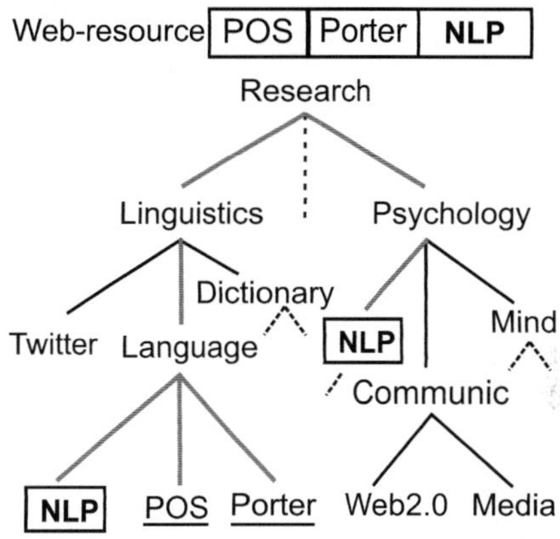

Figure 2: Example of Ambiguous Tags in the Ontology

Formally we define the density of the ontology T for the set of resources R, denoted $Dens(T, R)$, as the average density over all resources in R, as follows.

$$Dens(T,R) = \frac{1}{|R|}\sum_{r \in R} density(r,T)$$

where $density(r, T)$ denotes the density for the given resource r for the ontology T, defined as:

$$density(r,T) = \frac{nTags(r) - 1}{\text{argmin}_{i,j}\, dist(node(i,T), node(j,T))}$$

and $nTags(r)$ is the number of tags assigned to r, $node(k, T)$ is the node in T for the kth tag (assigned to r), and $dist(n1, n2)$ is the number of edges between nodes $n1$ and $n2$ in T. So the density for the given resource is essentially the inverse of the minimum distance among the tags assigned to it. We computed the density value for the ontology derived by our approach ('Ontology Enhanced with Wiki Concepts') and compared with the ontologies obtained by using only the resources (where a tag vector is presented by the stemmed terms in the resources to which the tag is assigned), and only the tags (where a tag vector is presented by the resource to which they were assigned). Figures 3 and 4 show the results, for the two datasets. For both datasets, the differences between the three ontologies were statistically significant (at p=0.05), indicating that the encyclopedia knowledge obtained from Wikipedia was indeed effective in deriving a semantically dense ontology.

Here, one observation is that the relative improvement was more significant for the "Frequent Set" than the "Long Tail Set". The reason is because frequent tags are generally more ambiguous than less frequent tags (as with words in general), therefore the effect of tag disambiguation by DSCBC was more salient, relatively, for the frequent tags.

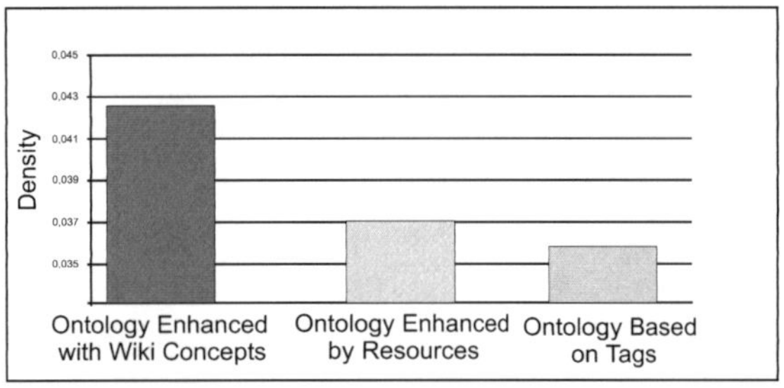

Figure 3: Ontological Density for "Frequent Set"

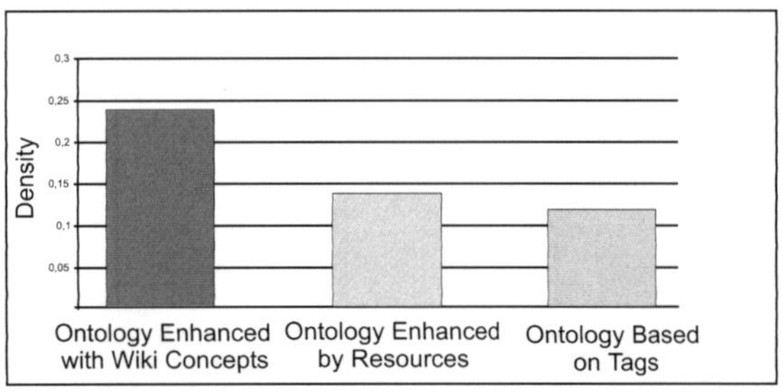

Figure 4: Ontological Density for "Long Tail Set"

5.3 Evaluation 2: Personalized Information Retrieval

For the second evaluation, we used the derived Delicious ontology in an IR task and measured its utility. In particular, we personalized the search results for a given user by utilizing the tag ontology as a way to present the user profile and infer his/her information needs.

Using the derived ontology, we search in the ontology for the query tag entered by a specific user. We first match the ontology with the user's profile and derive a score distribution for the nodes in the tree which reflects the user's general interest. To do so, we take each tag in the user's profile as the initial activation point, then spread the activation up and down the ontology tree, for all tags.

To spread activation from a given node, we use two parameters: *decay factor*, which determines the amount of the interest to be transfered to the parent/child of the current node; and *damping threshold* - if the interest score becomes less than this value we stop further iteration. Thus the resulting score distribution of the tree is effectively personalized to the user's general interest.

Using the obtained score distribution of a given user, we search the tree for a query tag (of this user). In the same way as the tags in the profile, we spread activation over the ontology from the node to which the tag belongs, but this time we add a weight to emphasize the relative importance of the query tag compared to the tags from the profile, because the query reflects the user's current information needs. Finally we feed the preference vector to the modified FolkRank algorithm (Hotho et al., 2006) to retrieve and rank the relevant web resources which reflect the user-specific preferences. Figure 5 shows the overall scheme of the personalized ranked retrieval using an ontological user profile.

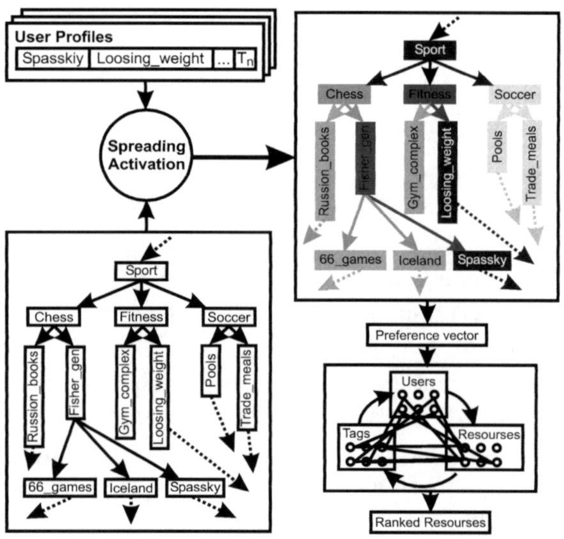

Figure 5: Ranked Retrieval in Folksonomies using Ontological User Profile

We evaluated the retrieval results by 5-fold cross validation. Given a test user profile, we used the leave-one-out method for tags – we removed a target tag from the user profile and treated it as a query. All resources which the user assigned with that tag was the relevant set. For the final results, we computed the F-score, which is defined as standard:

$$F = \frac{2 \cdot Precision \cdot Recall}{Precision + Recall}$$

Figure 6 and 7 show the F-scores for the two datasets. Note that 'TopN' indicates the top N retrieved resources. As you can see, the ontology enhanced with the Wiki concepts was able to better reflect the users' interest and produced significant improvements compared to the ontologies built only with the Delicious resources. Moreover, the improvements were much more significant for the "Long Tail Set" than the "Frequent Set", as consistent with our intuitions – Wikipedia's encyclopedia knowledge helped enhance the information about the less-frequent tags (assigned by the users with sparse profiles), thereby overcoming the "Cold Start" problem in search personalization.

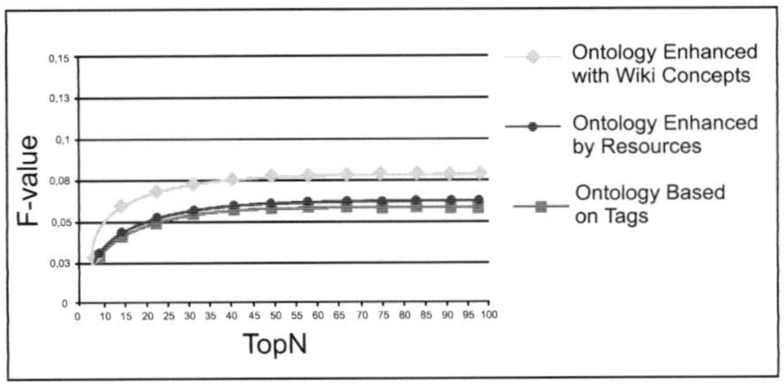

Figure 6: F-score of the Ontology for "Frequent Set"

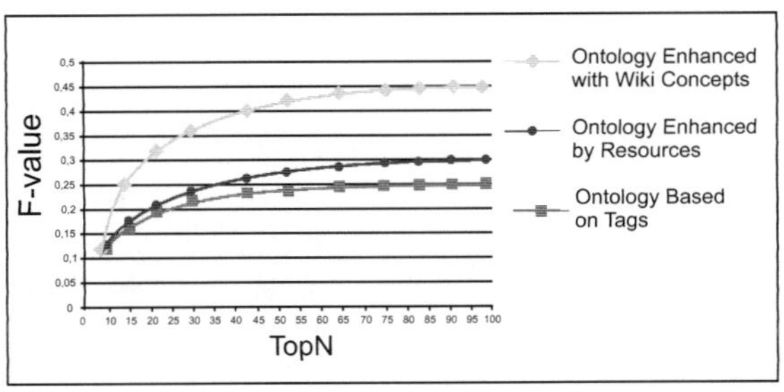

Figure 7: F-score of the Ontology for "Long Tail Set"

6 Conclusions and Future Work

In this paper, we presented a novel method for disambiguating tags and incorporating encyclopedia knowledge from Wikipedia in building folksonomy ontologies for social tagging systems. We applied our method to the data from Delicious and showed that, not only was the derived ontology semantically more dense (i.e., similar tags/concepts are clustered in close proximity), it also proved to be very effective in a search personalization task as well.

For future work, we are planning on investigating different ways of incorporating the link structures of Wikipedia and web pages in the tag similarity function (in DSCBC). Possible ideas include adding different weights on various types of links (or links appearing in various sections of a page/article), and using distance in the reachability relation, for example using the work done in Wikipedia Mining (Nakayama et al., 2008).

Finally, we are planning on applying information extraction or summarization techniques on Wikipedia articles to focus on sentences which provide relevant and important information about the subject.

References

D. Ahn, V. Jijkoun, G. Mishene, K. Muller, M. DeRijke, and S. Schlobach. 2004. Using Wikipedia at the TREC QA Track. In *Proceedings of the 13th Text Retrieval Conference (TREC 2004).*

P. Clough, H. Joho, and M. Sanderson. 2005. Automatically Organizing Images Using Concept Hierarchies. In *Proceedings of the SIGIR Workshop on Multimedia Information Retrieval.*

A. Culotta, A. Mccallum, and J.Betz. 2006. Integrating Probabilistic Extraction Models and Data Mining to Discover Relations and Patterns in Text. In *Proceedings of the Human Language Technology Conference.*

E. Gabrilovich and S. Markovitch. 2006. Overcoming the Brittleness Bottleneck Using Wikipedia: Enhancing Text Categorization with Encyclopedic Knowledge. In *Proceedings of the National Conference on Artificial Intelligence.*

I. Gurevych, C. Muler, and T. Zesch. 2007. What to be? - Electronic Career Guidance Based on Semantic Relatedness. In *Proceedings of the 45th Annual Meeting of the Association for Computational Linguistics.*

P. Heymann and H. Garcia-Molina. 2006. Collaborative Creation of Communal Hierarchical Taxonomies in Social Tagging Systems. Technical Report 2006-10, Computer Science Department, April.

A. Hotho, R. Jaschke, C. Schmitz, and G. Stumme. 2006. Folkrank: A Ranking Algorithm for Folksonomies. In *Proceedings of the FGIR*.

R. Mihalcea and A. Csomai. 2007. Wikify!: Linking Documents to Encyclopedic Knowledge. In *Proceedings of the sixteenth ACM conference on Conference on information and knowledge management*.

P. Mika. 2007. Ontologies Are Us: A Unified Model of Social Networks and Semantics. *Web Semantics: Science, Services and Agents on the World Wide Web*, 5(1).

G. Miller. 1990. WordNet: An Online Lexical Database. *International Journal of Lexicography*, 3(4).

D. Milne, O. Medelyan, and I. Witten. 2006. Mining Domain-Specific Thesauri from Wikipedia: A Case Study. In *Proceedings of the 2006 IEEE/WIC/ACM International Conference on Web Intelligence*.

K. Nakayama, T. Hara, and S. Nishio. 2008. Wikipedia Mining - Wikipedia as a Corpus for Knowledge Extraction. In *Proceedings of Annual Wikipedia Conference (Wikimania)*.

M. OConnor and J. Herlocker. 2001. Clustering Items for Collaborative Filtering. In *Proceedings of SIGIR-2001 Workshop on Recommender Systems*.

P. Pantel and D. Lin. 2002. Discovering Word Senses from Text. In *Proceedings of the 8th ACM Conference on Knowledge Discovery and Data Mining (KDD-02)*.

P. Schmitz. 2006. Inducing Ontology From Flickr Tags. In *Proceedings of the Collaborative Web Tagging Workshop (WWW 06)*.

A. Shepitsen, J. Gemmell, B. Mobasher, and R. Burke. 2008. Personalized Recommendation in Social Tagging Systems Using Hierarchical Clustering. In *Proceedings of the 2008 ACM conference on Recommender Systems*.

N. Tomuro, S. Lytinen, K. Kanzaki, and H. Isahara. 2007. Clustering Using Feature Domain Similarity to Discover Word Senses for Adjectives. In *Proceedings of the 1st IEEE International Conference on Semantic Computing (ICSC-2007)*.

Acquiring High Quality Non-Expert Knowledge from On-demand Workforce

Donghui Feng **Sveva Besana** **Remi Zajac**
AT&T Interactive Research
Glendale, CA, 91203
{dfeng, sbesana, rzajac}@attinteractive.com

Abstract

Being expensive and time consuming, human knowledge acquisition has consistently been a major bottleneck for solving real problems. In this paper, we present a practical framework for acquiring high quality non-expert knowledge from on-demand workforce using Amazon Mechanical Turk (MTurk). We show how to apply this framework to collect large-scale human knowledge on AOL query classification in a fast and efficient fashion. Based on extensive experiments and analysis, we demonstrate how to detect low-quality labels from massive data sets and their impact on collecting high-quality knowledge. Our experimental findings also provide insight into the best practices on balancing cost and data quality for using MTurk.

1 Introduction

Human knowledge acquisition is critical for training intelligent systems to solve real problems, both for industry applications and academic research. For example, many machine learning and natural language processing tasks require non-trivial human labeled data for supervised learning-based approaches. Traditionally this has been collected from domain experts, which we refer to as expert knowledge.

However, acquiring in-house expert knowledge is usually very expensive, time consuming, and has consistently been a major bottleneck for many research problems. For example, tremendous efforts have been put into creating TREC corpora (Voorhees, 2003).

As a result, several research projects sponsored by NSF and DARPA aim to construct valuable data resources via human labeling; these are exemplified by PennTree Bank (Marcus *et al.*, 1993), FrameNet (Baker *et al.,* 1998), and OntoNotes (Hovy *et al.*, 2006).

In addition, there are projects such as Open Mind Common Sense (OMCS) (Stork, 1999; Singh *et al.*, 2002), ISI LEARNER (Chklovski, 2003), and the Fact Entry Tool by Cycorp (Belasco *et al.*, 2002) where knowledge is gathered from volunteers.

One interesting approach followed by von Ahn and Dabbish (2004), applied to image labeling on the Web, is to collect valuable input from entertained labelers. Turning label acquisition into a computer game addresses tediousness, which is one of the main reasons that it is hard to gather large quantities of data from volunteers.

More recently researchers have begun to explore approaches for acquiring human knowledge from an on-demand workforce such as Amazon Mechanical Turk[1]. MTurk is a marketplace for jobs that require human intelligence.

There has been an increase in demand for crowdsourcing prompted by both the academic community and industry needs. For instance, Microsoft/Powerset uses MTurk for search relevance evaluation and other companies are leveraging turkers to clean their data sources.

However, while it is cheap and fast to obtain large-scale non-expert labels using MTurk, it is still unclear how to leverage its capability more efficiently and economically to obtain sufficient useful and high-quality data for solving real problems.

In this paper, we present a practical framework for acquiring high quality non-expert knowledge using MTurk. As a case study we have applied this framework to obtain human classifications on AOL queries (determining whether a query might be a local search or not). Based on extensive experiments and analysis, we show how to detect bad labelers/labels from massive data sets and how to build high-quality labeling sets. Our experiments also provide in-

[1] Amazon Mechanical Turk: http://www.mturk.com/

Proceedings of the 2009 Workshop on the People's Web Meets NLP, ACL-IJCNLP 2009, pages 51–56,
Suntec, Singapore, 7 August 2009.

sight into the best practices for balancing cost and data quality when using MTurk.

The remainder of this paper is organized as follows: In Section 2, we review related work using MTurk. We describe our methodology in Section 3 and in Section 4 we present our experimental results and further analysis. In Section 5 we draw conclusions and discuss our plans for future work.

2 Related Work

It is either infeasible or very time and cost consuming to acquire in-house expert human knowledge. To obtain valuable human knowledge (*e.g.*, in the format of labeled data), many research projects in the natural language community have been funded to create large-scale corpora and knowledge bases, such as PenTreeBank (Marcus *et al.*, 1993), FrameNet (Baker *et al.*, 1998), PropBank (Palmer *et al.*, 2005), and OntoNotes (Hovy *et al.*, 2006).

MTurk has been attracting much attention within several research areas since its release. Su *et al.* (2007) use MTurk to collect large-scale review data. Kaisser and Lowe (2008) report their work on generating research collections of question-answering pairs using MTurk. Sorokin and Forsyth (2008) outsource image-labeling tasks to MTurk. Kittur *et al.* (2008) use MTurk as the paradigm for user studies. In the natural language community Snow *et al.* (2008) report their work on collecting linguistic annotation for a variety of natural language tasks including word sense disambiguation, word similarity, and textual entailment recognition.

However, most of the reported work focuses on how to apply data collected from MTurk to their applications. In our work, we concentrate on presenting a practical framework for using MTurk by separating the process into a validation phase and a large-scale submission phase.

By analyzing workers' behavior and their data quality, we investigate how to detect low-quality labels and their impact on collected human knowledge; in addition, during the validation step we study how to best use MTurk to balance payments and data quality. Although our work is based on the submission of a classification task, the framework and approaches can be adapted for other types of tasks.

In the next section, we will discuss in more detail our practical framework for using MTurk.

3 Methodology

3.1 Amazon Mechanical Turk

Amazon launched their MTurk service in 2005. This service was initially used for internal projects and eventually fulfilled the demand for using human intelligence to perform various tasks that computers currently cannot do or do very well.

MTurk users naturally fall into two roles: a requester and a turker. As a requester, you can define your Human Intelligent Tasks (HITs), design suitable templates, and submit your tasks to be completed by turkers. A turker may choose from HITs that she is eligible to work on and get paid after the requester approves her work. The work presented in this paper is mostly from the perspective of a requester.

3.2 Key Issues

While it is quite easy to start using MTurk, requesters have to confront the following: how can we obtain sufficient useful and high-quality data for solving real problems efficiently and economically?

In practice, there are three key issues to consider when answering this question.

Key Issues	Description
Data Quality	Is the labeled data good enough for practical use?
Cost	What is the sweet spot for payment?
Scale	How efficiently can MTurk be used when handling large-scale data sets? Can the submitted job be done in a timely manner?

Table 1. Key issues for using MTurk.

Requesters want to obtain high-quality data on a large scale without overpaying turkers. Our proposed framework will address these key issues.

3.3 Approaches

Since not all tasks collecting non-expert knowledge share the same characteristics and suitable applications, there is not a one-size-fits-all solution as the best practice when using MTurk.

In our approach, we divide the process into two phases:

- Validation Phase.
- Large-scale Submission Phase.

The first phase gives us information used to determine if MTurk is a valid approach for a given problem and what the optimal parameters for high quality and a short turn-around time are.

We have to determine the right cost for the task and the optimal number of labels. We empirically determine these parameters with an MTurk submission using a small amount of data. These optimal parameters are then used for the large-scale submission phase.

Most data labeling tasks require subjective judgments. One cannot expect labeling results from different labelers to always be the same. The degree of agreement among turkers varies depending on the complexity and ambiguity of individual tasks. Typically we need to obtain multiple labels for each HIT by assigning multiple turkers to the same task.

Researchers mainly use the following two quantitative measures to assess inter-agreement: observed agreement and kappa statistics.

$P(A)$ is the observed agreement among annotators. It represents the portion where annotators produce identical labels. This is very natural and straightforward. However, people argue this may not necessarily reflect the exact degree of agreement due to chance agreement.

$P(E)$ is the hypothetical probability of chance agreement. In other words, $P(E)$ represents the degree of agreement if both annotators conduct annotations randomly (according to their own prior probability).

We can also use the kappa coefficient as a quantitative measure of inter-person agreement. It is a commonly used measure to remove the effect of chance agreement. It was first introduced in statistics (Cohen, 1960) and has been widely used in the language technology community, especially for corpus-driven approaches (Carletta, 1996; Krippendorf, 1980). Kappa is defined with the following equation:

$$kappa = \frac{P(A) - P(E)}{1 - P(E)}$$

Generally it is viewed more robust than observed agreement $P(A)$ because it removes chance agreement $P(E)$.

```
DetectOutlier( P )
  for each turker p ∈ P
    collect the label set L from p
    for each label l ∈ L
      /* compared with others' majority voting */
      compute its agreement with others
    compute P(A)_p (or kappa_p)
  analyze the distribution of P(A)
  return outlier turkers
```

Figure 1. Outlier detection algorithm.

We use these measures to automatically detect outlier turkers producing low-quality results. Figure 1 shows our algorithm for automatically detecting outlier turkers.

4 Experiments

Based on our proposed framework and approaches, as a case study we conducted experiments on a classification task using MTurk.

The classification task requires the turker to determine whether a web query is a local search or not. For example, is the user typing this query looking for a local business or not? The labeled data set can be used to train a query classifier for a web search system.

This capability will make search systems able to distinguish local search queries from other types of queries and to apply specific search algorithms and data resources to better serve users' information needs.

For example, if a person types "largest biomed company in San Diego" and the web search systems can recognize this query as a local search query, it will apply local search algorithms on listing data instead of or as well as generating a general web search request.

4.1 Validation Phase

We downloaded the publicly available AOL query log[2] and used this as our corpus. We first scanned all queries with geographic locations (including states, cities, and neighborhoods) and then randomly selected a set of queries for our experiments.

For the validation phase, 700 queries were first labeled in-house by domain experts and we refer to this set as expert labels. To obtain the optimal parameters including the desired number of labels and payment price, we designed our HITs and experiments in the following way:

We put 10 queries into one HIT, requested 15 labels for each query/HIT, and varied payment for each HIT in four separate runs. Our payments include \$0.01, \$0.02, \$0.05, and \$0.10 per HIT. The goal is to have HITs completed in a timely fashion and have them yield high-quality data.

We submitted our HITs to MTurk in four different runs with the following prices: \$0.01, \$0.02, \$0.03, and \$0.10. According to our predefined evaluation measures and our outlier detection algorithm, we investigated how to obtain the optimal parameters. Figure 2. shows the task completion statistics for the four different runs.

[2] AOL Log Data: http://www.gregsadetsky.com/aol-data/

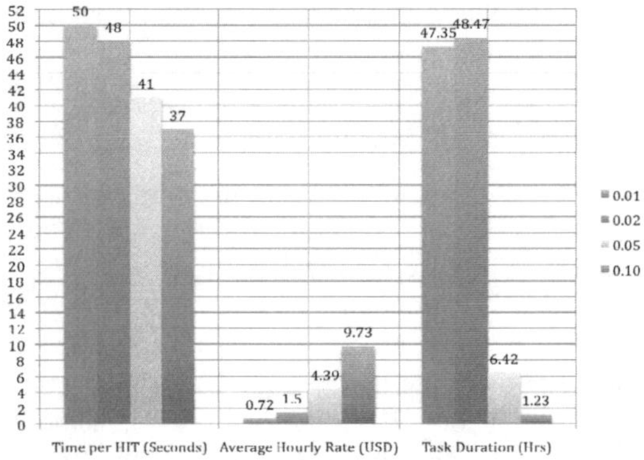

Figure 2. Task completion statistics.

As shown in Figure 2, with the increase of payments, the average hourly rate increases from \$0.72 to \$9.73 and the total turn-around time dramatically decreases from more than 47 hours to about 1.5 hours. In the meantime, people tend to become more focused on the tasks and spend less time per HIT.

In addition, as we increase payment, more people tend to stay with the task and take it more seriously as evidenced by the quality of the labeled data. This results in fewer numbers of workers overall as well as fewer outliers as shown in Figure 3.

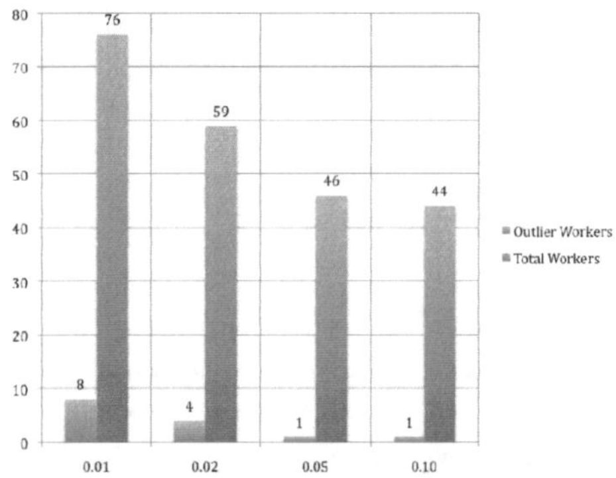

Figure 3. Total number of workers and outliers.

We investigate two types of agreements, inter-turker agreement and agreement between turkers and our in-house experts. For inter non-expert agreements, we compute each turker's agreement with all others' majority voting results.

Payment (USD)	0.01	0.02	0.05	0.10
Median of inter-turker agreement	0.8074	0.8583	0.9346	0.9028

Table 2. Median of inter-turker agreements.

As in our outlier detection algorithm, we analyzed the distribution of inter-turker agreements. Table 2 shows the median values of inter-turker agreement as we vary the payment prices. The median value keeps on increasing when the price increases from \$0.01, to \$0.02 and \$0.05. However, it drops as the price increases from \$0.05 to \$0.10. This implies that turkers do not necessarily improve their work quality as they get paid more. One of the possible explanations for this phenomenon is that when the reward is high people tend to work towards completing the task as fast as possible instead of focusing on submitting high-quality data. This trend may be intrinsic to the task we have submitted and further experiments will show if this turker behavior is task-independent.

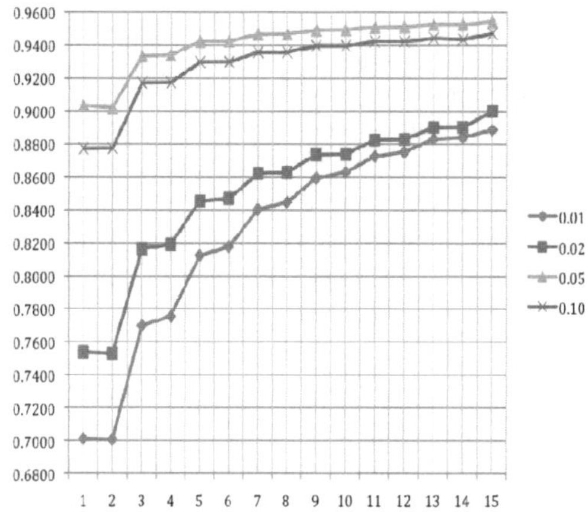

Figure 4. Agreement with experts.

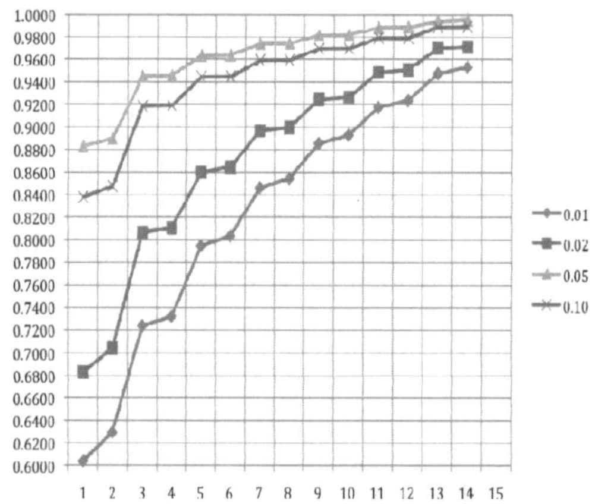

Figure 5. Inter non-expert agreement.

We also analyzed agreement between non-experts and experts. Figure 4 depicts the trend of the agreement scores with the increase of number of labels and payments. For example, given seven labels per query, in the experiment with the \$0.05 payment, the majority voting of non-expert labels has an agreement of 0.9465 with expert labeling. As explained earlier we do not necessarily obtain the best data quality/agreement with the \$0.10 payment. Instead, we get the highest agreement with the \$0.05 payment. We have determined this rate to be the sweet spot in terms of cost. Also, seven labels per query produce a very high agreement with no further significant improvement when we increase the number of labels.

For inter non-expert agreements, we found similar trends in terms of different payments and number of labels as shown in Figure 5.

As mentioned above, our algorithm is able to detect turkers producing low-quality data. One natural question is: how will their labels affect the overall data quality?

We studied this problem in two different ways. We evaluated the data quality by removing either all polluted queries or only outliers' labels. Here polluted queries refer to those queries receiving at least one label from outliers. By removing polluted queries, we only investigate the clean data set without any outlier labels. The other alternative is to only remove outliers' labels for specific queries but others' labels for those queries will be kept. Both the agreement between experts and non-experts and inter-non-experts agreement show similar trends: data quality without outliers' labels is slightly better since there is less noise. However, as outliers' labels may span a large number of queries, it may not be feasible to remove all polluted queries. For example, in one of our experiments, outliers' labels pollute more than half of all the records. We cannot simply remove all the queries with outliers' labels due to consideration of cost.

On the other hand, the effect of outliers' labels is not that significant if a certain number of requested labels per query are collected. As shown in Figure 6, noisy data from outliers can be overridden by assigning more labelers.

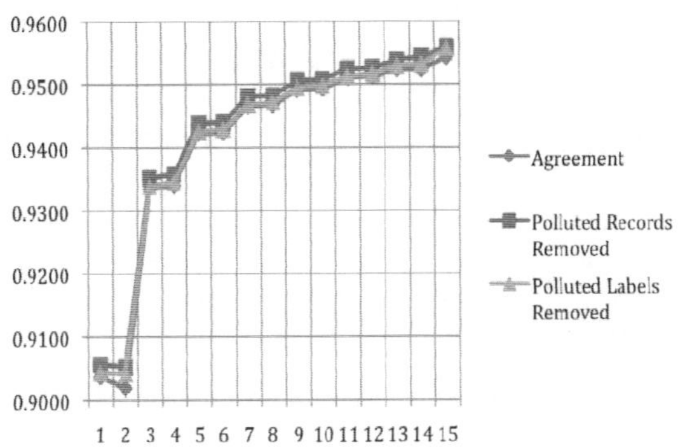

Figure 6. Agreement with Experts (removing outliers' labels (payment = $0.05)).

From the validation phase of the query classification task, we determine that the optimal parameters are paying $0.05 per HIT and requesting seven labels per query. Given this number of labels, the effect of outliers' labels can be overridden for the final result.

4.2 Large-scale Submission Phase

Having obtained the optimal parameters from the validation phase, we are then ready to make a large-scale submission.

For this phase, we paid $0.05 per HIT and requested seven labels per query/HIT. Following similar filtering and sampling approaches as in the validation phase, we selected 22.5k queries from the AOL search log. Table 3 shows the detected outliers for this large-scale submission.

Total Number of Turkers	228
Number of Outlier Turkers	23
Outlier Ratio	10.09%

Table 3. Number of turkers and outliers.

Based on the distribution of inter-turker agreement, any turkers with agreement less than 0.6501 are recognized as outliers. For a total number of 15,750 HITs, 228 turkers contributed to the labeling effort and 10.09% of them were recognized as outliers.

Table 4 shows the number of labels from the outliers and the approval ratio of collected data. About 10.08% of labels are from outlier turkers and rejected.

Total Number of Labels	157,500
Number of Outlier Labels	15,870
Approval Ratio	89.92%

Table 4. Total number of labels.

We have experimented using MTurk for a web query classification task. With learned optimal parameters from the validation phase, we collected large-scale high-quality non-expert labels in a fast and economical way. These data will be used to train query classifiers to enhance web search systems handling local search queries.

5 Conclusions and Future Work

In this paper, we presented a practical framework for acquiring high quality non-expert knowledge from an on-demand and scalable workforce. Using Amazon Mechanical Turk, we collected large-scale human classification knowledge on web search queries.

To learn the best practices when using MTurk, we presented a two-phase approach, a validation phase and a large-scale submission phase. We conducted extensive experiments to obtain the optimal parameters on the number of labelers and payments in the validation phase. We also presented an algorithm to automatically detect outlier turkers based on the agreement analysis and investigated the effect of removing an inaccurately labeled set.

Acquiring high-quality human knowledge will remain a major concern and a bottleneck for industry applications and academic problems. Unlike traditional ways of collecting in-house human knowledge, MTurk provides an alternative way to acquire non-expert knowledge. As shown in our experiments, given appropriate quality control, we have been able to acquire high-quality data in a very fast and efficient way. We believe MTurk will attract more attention and usage in broader areas.

In the future, we are planning to investigate how this framework can be applied to different types of human knowledge acquisition tasks and how to leverage large-scale labeled data sets for solving natural language processing problems.

References

Baker, C.F., Fillmore, C.J., and Lowe, J.B. 1998. The Berkeley FrameNet Project. In *Proc. of COLING-ACL-1998.*

Belasco, A., Curtis, J., Kahlert, R., Klein, C., Mayans, C., and Reagan, P. 2002. Representing Knowledge Gaps Effectively. In *Practical Aspects of Knowledge Management*, (*PAKM*).

Carletta, J. 1996. Assessing agreement on classification tasks: the kappa statistic. *Computational Linguistics*. 22(2):249–254.

Chklovski, T. 2003. LEARNER: A System for Acquiring Commonsense Knowledge by Analogy. In *Proc. of Second International Conference on Knowledge Capture (KCAP 2003).*

Cohen, J. 1960. A coefficient of agreement for nominal scales. *Educational and Psychological Measurement.* Vol.20, No.1, pp.37-46.

Colowick, S.M. and Pool, J. 2007. Disambiguating for the web: a test of two methods. In *Proc. of the 4th international Conference on Knowledge Capture (K-CAP 2007).*

Hovy, E., Marcus, M., Palmer, M., Ramshaw, L., and Weischedel, R. 2006. OntoNotes: The 90% Solution. In *Proc. of HLT-NAACL-2006.*

Kaisser, M. and Lowe, J.B. 2008. Creating a Research Collection of Question Answer Sentence Pairs with Amazon's Mechanical Turk. In *Proc. of the Fifth International Conference on Language Resources and Evaluation (LREC-2008).*

Kittur, A., Chi, E. H., and Suh, B. 2008. Crowdsourcing user studies with Mechanical Turk. In *Proc. of the 26th Annual ACM Conference on Human Factors in Computing Systems (CHI-2008).*

Krippendorf, K. 1980. *Content Analysis: An introduction to its methodology*. Sage Publications.

Marcus, M., Marcinkiewicz, M.A., and Santorini, B. 1993. Building a large annotated corpus of English: the Penn Treebank. *Computational Linguistics.* 19:2, June 1993.

Nakov, P. 2008. Paraphrasing Verbs for Noun Compound Interpretation. In *Proc. of the Workshop on Multiword Expressions (MWE-2008).*

Palmer, M., Gildea, D., and Kingsbury, P. 2005. The Proposition Bank: A Corpus Annotated with Semantic Roles. *Computational Linguistics.* 31:1.

Sheng, V.S., Provost, F., and Ipeirotis, P.G. 2008. Get another label? improving data quality and data mining using multiple, noisy labelers. In *Proc. of the 14th ACM SIGKDD international Conference on Knowledge Discovery and Data Mining (KDD-2008).*

Singh, P., Lin, T., Mueller, E., Lim, G., Perkins, T., and Zhu, W. 2002. Open Mind Common Sense: Knowledge acquisition from the general public. In Meersman, R. and Tari, Z. (Eds.), LNCS: Vol. 2519. *On the Move to Meaningful Internet Systems: DOA/CoopIS/ODBASE* (pp. 1223-1237). Springer-Verlag.

Snow, R., O'Connor, B., Jurafsky, D., and Ng, A.Y. 2008. Cheap and Fast – But is it Good? Evaluating Non-Expert Annotations for Natural Language Tasks . In *Proc. of EMNLP-2008.*

Sorokin, A. and Forsyth, D. 2008. Utility data annotation with Amazon Mechanical Turk. In *Proc. of the First IEEE Workshop on Internet Vision at CVPR-2008.*

Stork, D.G. 1999. The Open Mind Initiative. *IEEE Expert Systems and Their Applications.* pp. 16-20, May/June 1999.

Su, Q., Pavlov, D., Chow, J., and Baker, W.C. 2007. Internet-scale collection of human-reviewed data. In *Proc. of the 16th international Conference on World Wide Web (WWW-2007).*

Von Ahn, L. and Dabbish, L. 2004. Labeling Images with a Computer Game. In *Proc. of ACM Conference on Human Factors in Computing Systmes (CHI).* pp. 319-326.

Voorhees, E.M. 2003. Overview of TREC 2003. In *Proc. of TREC-2003.*

Constructing An Anaphorically Annotated Corpus With Non-Experts: Assessing The Quality Of Collaborative Annotations.

Jon Chamberlain
University of Essex
School of Computer Science
and Electronic Engineering
jchamb@essex.ac.uk

Udo Kruschwitz
University of Essex
School of Computer Science
and Electronic Engineering
udo@essex.ac.uk

Massimo Poesio
University of Essex
School of Computer Science
and Electronic Engineering
poesio@essex.ac.uk

Abstract

This paper reports on the ongoing work of *Phrase Detectives*, an attempt to create a very large anaphorically annotated text corpus. Annotated corpora of the size needed for modern computational linguistics research cannot be created by small groups of hand-annotators however the ESP game and similar *games with a purpose* have demonstrated how it might be possible to do this through Web collaboration. We show that this approach could be used to create large, high-quality natural language resources.

1 Introduction

The statistical revolution in natural language processing (NLP) has resulted in the first NLP systems and components really usable on a large scale, from part-of-speech (POS) taggers to parsers (Jurafsky and Martin, 2008). But it has also raised the problem of creating the large amounts of annotated linguistic data needed for training and evaluating such systems.

This requires trained annotators, which is prohibitively expensive both financially and in terms of person-hours (given the number of trained annotators available) on the scale required.

Recently, however, Web collaboration has started to emerge as a viable alternative. Wikipedia and similar initiatives have shown that a surprising number of individuals are willing to help with resource creation and scientific experiments. The goal of the ANAWIKI project[1] is to experiment with Web collaboration as a solution to the problem of creating large-scale linguistically annotated corpora. We do this by developing tools through which members of our scientific community can participate in corpus creation and by engaging non-expert volunteers with a game-like interface. In this paper we present ongoing work on *Phrase Detectives*[2], a game designed to collect judgments about anaphoric annotations, and we report a first analysis of annotation quality in the game.

2 Related Work

Large-scale annotation of low-level linguistic information (part-of-speech tags) began with the Brown Corpus, in which very low-tech and time consuming methods were used. For the creation of the British National Corpus (BNC), the first 100M-word linguistically annotated corpus, a faster methodology was developed using preliminary annotation with automatic methods followed by partial hand-correction (Burnard, 2000).

Medium and large-scale semantic annotation projects (for wordsense or coreference) are a recent innovation in Computational Linguistics. The semi-automatic annotation methodology cannot yet be used for this type of annotation, as the quality of, for instance, coreference resolvers is not yet high enough on general text. Nevertheless the semantic annotation methodology has made great progress with the development, on the one end, of effective quality control methods (Hovy et al., 2006) and on the other, of sophisticated annotation tools such as Serengeti (Stührenberg et al., 2007).

These developments have made it possible to move from the small-scale semantic annotation projects, the aim of which was to create resources of around 100K words in size (Poesio, 2004b), to the efforts made as part of US initiatives such as Automatic Context Extraction (ACE), Translingual Information Detection, Extraction and Summarization (TIDES), and GALE to create 1 million word corpora. Such techniques could not be expected to annotate data on the scale of the BNC.

[1] http://www.anawiki.org

[2] http://www.phrasedetectives.org

Proceedings of the 2009 Workshop on the People's Web Meets NLP, ACL-IJCNLP 2009, pages 57–62,
Suntec, Singapore, 7 August 2009.

2.1 Collaborative Resource Creation

Collaborative resource creation on the Web offers a different solution to this problem. The motivation for this is the observation that a group of individuals can contribute to a collective solution, which has a better performance and is more robust than an individual's solution as demonstrated in simulations of collective behaviours in self-organizing systems (Johnson et al., 1998).

Wikipedia is perhaps the best example of collaborative resource creation, but it is not an isolated case. The gaming approach to data collection, termed *games with a purpose*, has received increased attention since the success of the ESP game (von Ahn, 2006).

2.2 Human Computation

Human computation, as a more general concept than *games with a purpose*, has become popular in numerous research areas. The underlying assumption of learning from a vast user population has been largely the same in each approach. Users are engaged in different ways to achieve objectives such as:

- Assigning labels to items
- Learning to rank
- Acquiring structured knowledge

An example of the first category is the ESP game which was a project to label images with tags through a competitive game. 13,500 users played the game, creating 1.3M labels in 3 months (von Ahn, 2006). Other examples of assigning lables to items include Phetch and Peekaboom (von Ahn et al., 2006).

Learning to rank is a very different objective. For example user judgements are collected in the *Picture This* game (Bennett et al., 2009). This is a two player game where the user has to select the best matching image for a given query from a small set of potential candidates. The aim is to learn a preference ranking from the user votes to predict the preference of future users. Several methods for modeling the collected preferences confirmed the assumption that a consensus ranking from one set of users can be used to model another.

Phrase Detectives is in the third category, i.e. it aims to acquire structured knowledge, ultimately

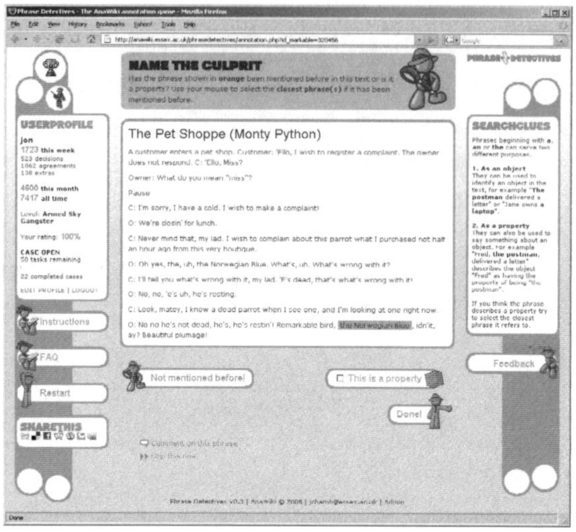

Figure 1: A screenshot of the Annotation Mode.

leading to a linguistically annotated corpus. Another example of aiming to acquire large amounts of structured knowledge is the Open Mind Commonsense project, a project to mine commonsense knowledge to which 14,500 participants contributed nearly 700,000 sentences (Singh, 2002).

Current efforts in attempting to acquire large-scale world knowledge from Web users include Freebase[3] and True Knowledge[4]. A slightly different approach to the creation of commonsense knowledge has been pursued in the Semantic MediaWiki project (Krötzsch et al., 2007), an effort to develop a 'Wikipedia way to the Semantic Web': i.e., to make Wikipedia more useful and to support improved search of web pages via semantic annotation.

3 The Phrase Detectives game

Phrase Detectives offers a simple graphical user interface for non-expert users to learn how to annotate text and to make annotation decisions (Chamberlain et al., 2008).

In order to use Web collaboration to create annotated data, a number of issues have to be addressed. First among these is motivation. For anybody other than a few truly dedicated people, annotation is a very boring task. This is where the promise of the game approach lies. Provided that a suitably entertaining format can be found, it may be possible to get people to tag quite a lot of data without them even realizing it.

[3] `http://www.freebase.com/`

[4] `http://www.trueknowledge.com/`

The second issue is being able to recruit sufficient numbers of useful players to make the results robust. Both of these issues have been addressed in the incentive structures of Phrase Detectives (Chamberlain et al., 2009).

Other problems still remain, most important of which is to ensure the *quality* of the annotated data. We have identified four aspects that need to be addressed to control annotation quality:

- Ensuring users understand the task
- Attention slips
- Malicious behaviour
- Genuine ambiguity of data

These issues have been addressed at the design stage of the project (Kruschwitz et al., 2009).

The goal of the game is to identify relationships between words and phrases in a short text. An example of a task would be to highlight an anaphor-antecedent relation between the markables (sections of text) *'This parrot'* and *'He'* in *'This parrot is no more! He has ceased to be!'* Markables are identified in the text by automatic pre-processing. There are two ways to annotate within the game: by selecting a markable that corefers to another one (Annotation Mode); or by validating a decision previously submitted by another player (Validation Mode).

Annotation Mode (see Figure 1) is the simplest way of collecting judgments. The player has to locate the closest antecedent markable of an anaphor markable, i.e. an earlier mention of the object. By moving the cursor over the text, markables are revealed in a bordered box. To select it the player clicks on the bordered box and the markable becomes highlighted. They can repeat this process if there is more than one antecedent markable (e.g. for plural anaphors such as *'they'*). They submit the annotation by clicking the *Done!* button. The player can also indicate that the highlighted markable has not been mentioned before (i.e. it is not anaphoric), that it is non-referring (for example, *'it'* in *'Yeah, well it's not easy to pad these Python files out to 150 lines, you know.'*) or that it is the property of another markable (for example, *'a lumberjack'* being a property of *'I'* in *'I wanted to be a lumberjack!'*).

In Validation Mode (see Figure 2) the player is presented with an annotation from a previous

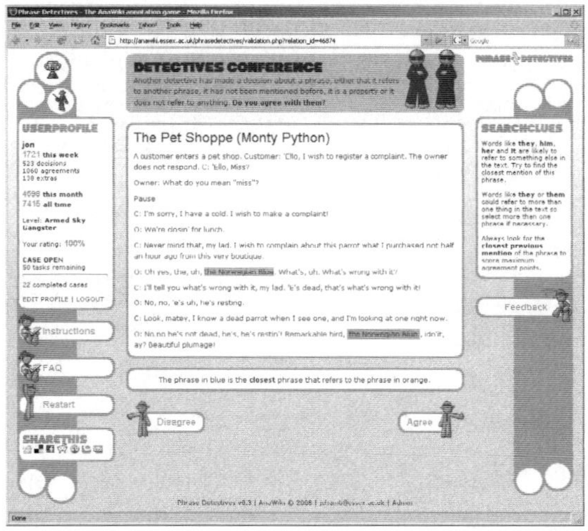

Figure 2: A screenshot of the Validation Mode.

player. The anaphor markable is shown with the antecedent markable(s) that the previous player chose. The player has to decide if he agrees with this annotation. If not he is shown the Annotation Mode to enter a new annotation.

In the game groups of players work on the same task over a period of time as this is likely to lead to a collectively intelligent decision (Surowiecki, 2005). An initial group of players are asked to annotate a markable. If all the players agree with each other then the markable is considered complete.

However it is likely that the first group of players will not agree with each other (62% of markables are given more than one relationship). In this case each unique relationship for the markable is validated by another group of players. This type of validation has also been proposed elsewhere, e.g. (Krause and Aras, 2009).

When the users register they begin with the training phase of the game. Their answers are compared with Gold Standard texts to give them feedback on their decisions and to get a user rating, which is used to determine whether they need more training. Contextual instructions are also available during the game.

The corpus used in the game is created from short texts including, for example, Wikipedia articles selected from the 'Featured Articles' and the page of 'Unusual Articles'; stories from Project Gutenberg including Aesop's Fables, Sherlock Holmes and Grimm's Fairy Tales; and dialogue texts from Textfile.com.

	Expert 1 vs. Expert 2	Expert 1 vs. Game	Expert 2 vs. Game
Overall agreement	94.1%	84.5%	83.9%
DN agreement	93.9%	96.0%	93.1%
DO agreement	93.3%	72.7%	70.0%
NR agreement	100.0%	100.0%	100.0%
PR agreement	100.0%	0.0%	0.0%

Table 1: Agreement figures for overall, discourse-new (DN), discourse-old (DO), non-referring (NR) and property (PR) attributes.

4 Results

The first public version of *Phrase Detectives* went live in December 2008. 1.1 million words have been converted and made ready for annotation. Over 920 players have submitted more than 380,000 annotations and validations of anaphoric relations. 46 documents have been fully annotated, meaning that at least 8 players have expressed their judgment on each markable, and each distinct anaphoric relation that these players assigned has been checked by four more players.

To put this in perspective, the GNOME corpus, produced by traditional methods, included around 3,000 annotations of anaphoric relations (Poesio, 2004a) whereas OntoNotes[5] 3.0, with 1 million words, contains around 140,000 annotations.

4.1 Agreement on annotations

A set of tools were developed to examine the decisions of the players, and address the following questions:

- How do the collective annotations produced by the game compare to annotations assigned by an expert annotator?
- What is the agreement between two experts annotating the same texts?

The answer to the first question will tell us whether the game is indeed successful at obtaining anaphoric annotations collaboratively within the game context. Anaphoric annotations are however considered much harder than other tasks such as part-of-speech tagging. Therefore we ask the second question which will give us an upper bound of what can be expected from the game in the best possible case.

We analysed five completed documents from the Wikipedia corpus containing 154 markables.

[5] http://www.ldc.upenn.edu

We first looked at overall agreement and then broke it down into individual types of anaphoric relations. The following types of relation can be assigned by players:

- DN (discourse-new): this markable has no anaphoric link to any previous markable.
- DO (discourse-old): this markable has an anaphoric link and the player needs to link it to the most recent antecedent.
- NR (non-referring): this markable does not refer to anything e.g. pleonistic "it".
- PR (property attribute): this markable represents a property of a previously mentioned markable.

DN is the most common relation with 70% of all markables falling in this category. 20% of markables are DO and form a coreference chain with markables previously mentioned. Less than 1% of markables are non-referring. The remaining markables have been identified as property attributes.

Each document was also manually annotated individually by two experts. Overall, we observe 84.5% agreement between Expert 1 and the game and 83.9% agreement between Expert 2 and the game. In other words, in about 84% of all cases the relation obtained from the majority vote of non-experts was identical to the one assigned by an expert. Table 1 gives a detailed breakdown of pairwise agreement values.

The agreement between the two experts is higher than between an expert and the game. This on its own is not surprising. However, an indication of the difficulty of the annotation task is the fact that the experts only agree in 94% of all cases. This can be seen as an upper boundary of what we might get out of the game.

Furthermore, we see that the figures for DN are very similar for all three comparisons. This seems to be the easiest type of relation to be detected.

DO relations appear to be more difficult to detect. However if we relax the DO agreement condition and do not check what the antecedent is, we get agreement figures above 90% in all cases: almost 97% between the two experts and between 91% and 93% when comparing an expert with the game. A number of these cases which are assigned as DO but with different antecedents are actually coreference chains which link to the same object. Extracting coreference chains from the game is part of the future work.

Although non-referring markables are rare, they are correctly identified in every case. We additonally checked every completed markable identified as NR in the corpus and found that there was 100% precision in 54 cases.

Property (PR) relations are very hard to identify and not a single one resulted from the game.

4.2 Disagreement on annotations

Disagreements between experts and the game were examined to understand whether the game was producing a poor quality annotation or whether the markable was in fact ambiguous. These are cases where the gold standard as created by an expert is not the interpretation derived from the game.

- In 60% of all cases where the game proposed a relation different from the expert annotation, the expert marked this relation to be a possible interpretation as well. In other words, the majority of disagreements are not false annotations but alternatives such as ambiguous interpretations or references to other markables in the same coreference chain. If we counted these cases as correct, we get an agreement ratio of above 93%, close to pairwise expert agreement.

- In cases of disagreement the relation identified by the expert was typically the second or third highest ranked relation in the game.

- The cumulative score of the expert relation (as calculated by the game) in cases of disagreement was 4.5, indicating strong player support for the expert relation even though it wasn't the top answer. A relation with a score of zero would be interpreted as one that has as many players supporting it as it has players disagreeing.

4.3 Discussion

There are very promising results in the agreement between an expert and the top answer produced from the game. By ignoring property relations and the identification of coreference chains, the results are close to what is expected from an expert. The particular difficulty uncovered by this analysis is the correct identification of properties attributes.

The analysis of markables with disagreement show that some heuristics and filtering should be applied to extract the highest quality decisions from the game. In many of the cases the game recorded plausible interpretations of different relations, which is valuable information when exploring more difficult and ambiguous markables. These would also be the markables that automatic anaphora resolution systems would have difficulty solving.

The data that was used to generate the results was not filtered in any way. It would be possible to ignore annotations from users who have a low rating (judged when players annotate a gold standard text). Annotation time could also be a factor in filtering the results. On average an annotation takes 9 seconds in Annotation Mode and 11 seconds in Validation Mode. Extreme variation from this may indicate that a poor quality decision has been made.

A different approach could be to identify those users who have shown to provide high quality input. A knowledge source could be created based on input from these users and ignore everything else. Related work in this area applies ideas from citation analysis to identify users of high expertise and reputation in social networks by, e.g., adopting Kleinberg's HITS algorithm (Yeun et al., 2009) or Google's PageRank (Luo and Shinaver, 2009).

The influence of document type may have a significant impact on both the distribution of markable types as well as agreement between experts and the game. We have only analysed the Wikipedia documents, however discourse texts from Gutenberg may provide different results.

5 Conclusions

This first detailed analysis of the annotations collected from a collaborative game aiming at a large anaphorically annotated corpus has demonstrated that high-quality natural language resources can be collected from non-expert users. A game approach can therefore be considered as a possible alternative to expert annotations.

We expect that the finally released corpus will apply certain heuristics to address the cases of disagreement between experts and consensus derived from the game.

6 Future Work

This paper has focused on percentage agreement between experts and the game output but this is a very simplistic approach. Various alternative agreement coefficients have been proposed that correct for chance agreement. One such measure is Cohen's κ (Cohen, 1960) which we are using to perform a more indepth analysis of the data.

The main part of our future work remains the creation of a very large annotated corpus. To achieve this we are converting source texts to include them in the game (our aim is a 100M word corpus). We have already started converting texts in different languages to be included in the next version of the game.

Acknowledgments

ANAWIKI is funded by a grant from the Engineering and Physical Sciences Research Council (EPSRC), grant number EP/F00575X/1. Thanks to Daniela Goecke, Nils Diewald, Maik Stührenberg and Daniel Jettka (University of Bielefeld), Mark Schellhase (University of Essex) and all the players who have contributed to the project

References

P. N. Bennett, D. M. Chickering, and A. Mityagin. 2009. Learning consensus opinion: mining data from a labeling game. In *Proceedings of the 18th International World Wide Web Conference (WWW2009)*, pages 121–130, Madrid.

L. Burnard. 2000. The British National Corpus Reference guide. Technical report, Oxford University Computing Services, Oxford.

J. Chamberlain, M. Poesio, and U. Kruschwitz. 2008. Phrase Detectives - A Web-based Collaborative Annotation Game. In *Proceedings of I-Semantics*, Graz.

J. Chamberlain, M. Poesio, and U. Kruschwitz. 2009. A new life for a dead parrot: Incentive structures in the Phrase Detectives game. In *Proceedings of the Webcentives Workshop at WWW'09*, Madrid.

J. Cohen. 1960. A coefficient of agreement for nominal scales. *Educational and Psychological Measurement*, 20(1):37–46.

E. Hovy, M. Marcus, M. Palmer, L. Ramshaw, and R. Weischedel. 2006. OntoNotes: The 90% Solution. In *Proceedings of HLT-NAACL06*.

N. L. Johnson, S. Rasmussen, C. Joslyn, L. Rocha, S. Smith, and M. Kantor. 1998. Symbiotic Intelligence: Self-Organizing Knowledge on Distributed Networks Driven by Human Interaction. In *Proceedings of the Sixth International Conference on Artificial Life*. MIT Press.

D. Jurafsky and J. H. Martin. 2008. *Speech and Language Processing- 2nd edition*. Prentice-Hall.

M. Krause and H. Aras. 2009. Playful tagging folksonomy generation using online games. In *Proceedings of the 18th International World Wide Web Conference (WWW2009)*, pages 1207–1208, Madrid.

M. Krötzsch, D. Vrandečič, M. Völkel, H. Haller, and R. Studer. 2007. Semantic Wikipedia. *Journal of Web Semantics*, 5:251–261.

U. Kruschwitz, J. Chamberlain, and M. Poesio. 2009. (Linguistic) Science Through Web Collaboration in the ANAWIKI Project. In *Proceedings of WebSci'09*, Athens.

X. Luo and J. Shinaver. 2009. MultiRank: Reputation Ranking for Generic Semantic Social Networks. In *Proceedings of the WWW 2009 Workshop on Web Incentives (WEBCENTIVES'09)*, Madrid.

M. Poesio. 2004a. Discourse annotation and semantic annotation in the gnome corpus. In *Proceedings of the ACL Workshop on Discourse Annotation*.

M. Poesio. 2004b. The MATE/GNOME scheme for anaphoric annotation, revisited. In *Proceedings of SIGDIAL*.

P. Singh. 2002. The public acquisition of commonsense knowledge. In *Proceedings of the AAAI Spring Symposium on Acquiring (and Using) Linguistic (and World) Knowledge for Information Access*, Palo Alto, CA.

M. Stührenberg, D. Goecke, N. Diewald, A. Mehler, and I. Cramer. 2007. Web-based annotation of anaphoric relations and lexical chains. In *Proceedings of the ACL Linguistic Annotation Workshop*, pages 140–147.

J. Surowiecki. 2005. *The Wisdom of Crowds*. Anchor.

L. von Ahn, R. Liu, and M. Blum. 2006. Peekaboom: a game for locating objects in images. In *Proceedings of CHI '06*, pages 55–64.

L. von Ahn. 2006. Games with a purpose. *Computer*, 39(6):92–94.

C. A. Yeun, M. G. Noll, N. Gibbins, C. Meinel, and N. Shadbolt. 2009. On Measuring Expertise in Collaborative Tagging Systems. In *Proceedings of WebSci'09*, Athens.

Author Index

Balasuriya, Dominic, 10
Besana, Sveva, 51
Brew, Chris, 28

Chamberlain, Jon, 57
Curran, James R., 10, 38

Feng, Donghui, 51
Fosler-Lussier, Eric, 28

Gantner, Zeno, 32
Gaume, Bruno, 19

Honnibal, Matthew, 38
Hsieh, ShuKai, 19
Huang, Chu-Ren, 19

Iria, Jose, 1

Kruschwitz, Udo, 57
Kuo, Ivy, 19

Magistry, Pierre, 19
Murphy, Tara, 10

Navarro, Emmanuel, 19
Nothman, Joel, 10, 38

Poesio, Massimo, 57
Prévot, Laurent, 19

Ringland, Nicky, 10

Sajous, Franck, 19
Schmidt-Thieme, Lars, 32
Shepitsen, Andriy, 42

Tomuro, Noriko, 42

Weale, Timothy, 28

Zajac, Remi, 51
Zhang, Ziqi, 1

Association for Computational Linguistics
209 N. Eighth Street
Stroudsburg, Pennsylvania 18360